THE BOYS UP NORTH

also by Paul Pintarich
History by the Glass

The Boys Up North

Dick Erath and the early Oregon winemakers

by PAUL PINTARICH

THE WYATT GROUP

Publishers 1997

ISBN 0-9656082-6-3

Published by The Wyatt Group, Portland, Oregon
Edited by Suzan Hall
Photographs on page 74 and 79 by John Rizzo.
Photograph on page 100 by Lou Manna, Inc.
All others from the Erath family archives.

Printed in Korea

Table of Contents

Foreword

by NEIL GOLDSCHMIDT

Look with favor upon a bold beginning.
VIRGIL

If you have ever been invited to write about something that you are certain is interesting but know that you don't write well enough to cap-
ture the essence, value and import of it, and you badly want to excite
the reader to want to read more, then you will sympathize with my
problem. That is exactly how I feel about trying to connect every wine-
loving prospective reader to *The Boys Up North: Dick Erath and the
early Oregon winemakers*. If you love wine, the lore of how it came to
be made, and stories about those without whom it wouldn't be the
same, at least in Oregon, then this book is your kind of fun. See what
I mean? The way I tell it, you might never have read this book.

In most career-threatening situations like this, I bail out by saying,
"You had to be there." But in this one, you actually still can "be there."
Paul Pintarich's stories let you meet and enjoy a cast of characters who
have made Oregon and American wine life more flavorful and a lot
more fun. Even better, most of these "heroes of Pinot" are still alive
and breaking new ground as you read. They can still be found at
Nick's, the IPNC, and, best of all, in their vineyards and cellars
reaching for a better clone and a better wine for us to drink, while
sharing most of what they know and believe with almost all comers.

As a law student in the middle-to-late 1960s, I fell in love with the
pastoral, ordered beauty of Napa Valley and the tasting rooms at
B.V., Beringer, Charles Krug, Inglenook, et al, where the wine was
priced right for a student. The traffic was light, and the men and
women selling their products in the tasting rooms were often part of
a small family of visionaries who believed they could compete with

the world's best. It wasn't arrogant, and they weren't pretentious; and that valley, with its talents and dreams, has pretty much fulfilled its great vision.

Oregon's founders are well on their way to the same accomplishment. But count yourself fortunate; you can still fly/drive/cycle out to Yamhill County and be part of their still-building dream. David Lett, while finding time to introduce Pinot Gris to his and Oregon's wine lands, is still fighting as a citizen volunteer for better land use planning in Oregon; so is Bill Blosser, in his role as chair of Oregon's most important state board for saving agricultural and forest land. David Adelsheim has been Oregon's unofficial ambassador to Burgundy, a relationship that has brought his home industry investment and, best of all, an exchange of valued ideas, clones and friendships. Apparently, winning winemaking awards was not enough to contain Dick Ponzi's irrepressible energy, so he has been busy helping found and build the microbrewery industry as a companion to a great wine story. Fuller, Redford, Sommer — all are still vital and contributing to this amazing "little state in the Northwest does good" legend.

Since this tale could not be woven centrally around the lives of all the people it includes, it is right and fun that it centers on Dick Erath, a generous, optimistic man who has given his full measure to assure Oregon's place on the world wine map. Everyone Dick Erath has touched has been left with a smile and a feeling of good fortune. His name is on his bottles, his place in history is secure, and he finally has a little time for golf with his friends. One might expect to find him handing off Erath's wine future to hired hands. Not yet; maybe not ever. He is too close to his land, his neighbors, and fulfilling his dream of the perfect bottle of his wine to be ready to pass on his torch.

I feel fortunate to have met and known many of the central figures in the story Paul Pintarich writes. Dick Erath and his fellow founders, Lett, Adelsheim, Ponzi, Redford, Bill Blosser and Susan Sokol-Blosser, have enriched my life, as they have the lives of so many others. Now Ken Wright, Paul Hart, and the Drouhin-Hatcher team have joined this march, as so many more will as the years pass.

What a grand thirty-or-so years; so much done in such a short time.

These wine pioneers have literally put us on the world map. Virgil would like this bold beginning. Thanks to Paul Pintarich for the memories — and for the reminder of our good fortune to have such passion and achievement alive among us.

Introduction

My grandfather, Paul J. Pintarich, was by avocation a Willamette Valley
winemaker. He had acquired the skill from my great-grandfather,
Matthew, who was a viticulturist near Zagreb in the Old Country of
Croatia. Grandpa's profession was custom tailoring, a craft he
had practiced in the Austro-Hungarian Army, and it earned him high
regard among Portland's better-dressed men for nearly fifty years.
Yet for him, as for many mustachioed gents in the city's once distinctive ethnic enclaves, winemaking was not only a consuming hobby
but the means of sustaining his cultural identity.

In the warm and lingering late summer, always the best time of year
in Western Oregon, Grandpa and his cronies would gather under the
grape arbor at the rear of the house. After lubricating their nostalgia
with Grandpa's wine, they would unlimber their *tambouritzas* and
sing songs of sweet Slavic sadness. At larger gatherings, like the annual
Croatian Fraternal Union picnic and lamb roast, much greater quantities of homemade wine flowed from the jugs of Portland's volatile
Croatians. Often, as the day wore on, there were grand melees over
minor slights, like who really won the three-legged race. Then my
grandfather, who was president of the union's Portland chapter, would
discreetly load the family onto the streetcar and wisely depart.

Unlike many of Portland's old-time winemakers, who purchased
grapes off railroad cars rolled up from California each fall, Grandpa
grew his own. The vines covered two sides of the family home in
Southwest Portland, where he also had his tailor shop and where my
father, Paul E. Pintarich, was born and still lives. Grandpa was skilled

at grafting and produced four grape varieties on his small lot: White Concord, Oregon Sweetwater, Riesling, and "Croatian Blues," a large, juicy, sweet, purple table variety he had brought from the Old Country. He made his wine in the basement, crushing the grapes in a press made by my late Uncle Mark, a cabinet maker, with leverage provided by an old automobile jack. The vintage was aged in two small oaken barrels previously occupied by whiskey. One barrel held a dark red wine. The other contained a pinkish-orange, Kool-aid-like substance everyone guessed was rosé.

On Sundays and holidays, when the family gathered at Grandpa's house as Old Country families used to do, Grandpa would bring his wine to the table in elegant, cut-glass decanters. Even my cousins and I, little kids then, were served glasses from Grandpa's hand. All of us joined in the traditional toast: "*Ziveli!*" Later in the day, we could find our fathers and uncles by following the cigarette smoke leaking from beneath the basement door. Putting our ears against the wood, we strained to understand the jokes they told in Serbo-Croatian as they smoked and drank.

Though Grandpa's vines have been neglected for many years, some whites and Croatian blues still survive. They are favored by the raccoon families, who strip the arbor each fall with remarkable speed and acrobatic skill. Visiting my father, I sometimes step downstairs and sniff the ancient, acrid odors of sour wine — tangible memories of my grandfather lingering in the basement, probably forever.

When I began writing this book, my mind filled with romantic memories of Grandpa and the old days. I asked my father, himself a less than successful winemaker in one period of his life, "So, Dad, be honest. What was Grandpa's wine really like?"

"Your grandpa," he said, without stirring in his lounger, "made terrible wine. And he made it out of anything, even Grandma's grape jam. And he bottled it in any kind of containers he could find, even old syrup bottles. I remember once..."

My older cousin Madalyn, whose memory is longer than mine, simply laughed. "You know the best thing about those *tambouritza* parties in the backyard?" she said. "Grandma's desserts. Grandpa always thought he could make wine, yet he fooled nobody. But everyone knew Grandma could cook."

So much for family mythology.

And so much for the "good old days" of Oregon winemaking. Back then, even suggesting the select grape varieties that now distinguish this state's renowned young wine industry would have caused out-of-state winemakers, especially those toiling in the established vineyards of Northern California, to roll their eyes.

In our provincial past, wine was a garish, screw-topped beverage reserved for special occasions or identified with a demimonde of winos, beatniks and lower-class ethnic families like my own. As a young serviceman and student who consumed considerable quantities of beer and spirits in the late 1950s and early '60s, I can testify that drinking wine, at least to me and my companions, was a small step above Sterno, shaving lotion, and the alcohol used in Naval torpedoes.

Wine was an experience shared out of a twisted brown paper bag, or the stuff Grandpa made, or the contents of that sticky, never quite empty bottle of purple Manischewitz under the sink. Or it was jugs of sometimes cloudy, always sweet-but-pleasant rhubarb, fruit, or berry wine from Henry Endres' venerable (founded 1936) farmer's winery in Oregon City.

In those days, Henry's epitomized the "wine experience" for many. With frivolous disregard we roared off to the winery, which was within drag-racing distance of Portland, skidded in, and complied with the "Honk for Service" sign. Usually someone would be there, exchanging jugs for cash through the little window. Sometimes, though, there would be a sign: "Gone Fishin'. Come back in the spring." Henry's may have lacked complexity, but the price was right — and it always had a finish.

Then things began to change.

By the late 1960s, ordinary people were suddenly drinking more and better wines, inadvertently participating in a gustatory renaissance that, during the following decade, was labeled "The Wine Rush Era." Its advent encouraged the beginnings of Oregon's modern wine industry.

Why this happened so dramatically is anybody's guess.

One probable cause was the emergence of an affluent, better-educated, broadly traveled generation of Americans. They returned from overseas infected with the "…after they've seen Paree" syndrome and its accompanying desire for more interesting food and wine. In addition, many American suburbanites were searching for sources of aesthetic enrichment to their clichéd lifestyle. The thing called "wine," with its easily accessible precocities of sipping, sniffing and endless, arcane chatter, was a means to the "hip, slick, and cool" necessary to escape an aspic of cultural ennui.

While dilettantes rose to the lure of the grape, a new breed of more serious aficionados was developing. Among them was the small group whose combined knowledge, dedication, and daring would, over the next twenty-five years, create Oregon's modern wine industry. As one Oregon winemaker put it, "We wanted to make our own foolishness."

Within a few years of their arrival in the Willamette Valley, these wine pioneers were winning national accolades for their winemaking skills. Not long after, they were earning international recognition for Pinot Noirs comparable to the legendary Burgundies of France. Richard Sommer of Hillcrest Valley Vineyard, a loner who came to the Umpqua Valley in 1961 and is considered "the father of the modern Oregon wine industry," refers to these friends and colleagues as "the boys up north."

For the purposes of this history, *The Boys Up North* include: Richard Erath (*Erath Vineyards*, 1968); Dick's former partner, C. Calvert "Cal" Knudsen; Charles Coury (*Coury Vineyards* 1967-78); Dave Lett (*The Eyrie Vineyards*, 1966); Richard Ponzi (*Ponzi Vineyards*, 1970); David Adelsheim (*Adelsheim Vineyard*, 1971); Bill Fuller (*Tualatin Vineyards*, 1973); Myron Redford (*Amity Vineyards*, 1974); and Bill Blosser (*Sokol Blosser Winery*, 1971). These men's memories provide insights into the past and future of Oregon's wine industry.

For the full Oregon wine story, other voices must be heard as well, especially: Richard Sommer, Pied Piper to many Oregon winemakers; grape growers Jim Maresh and his neighbor Arthur Weber; Rob Stuart, Dick Erath's winemaker; Barney Watson, winemaker and Senior Instructor of Enology at Oregon State University; Karen Hinsdale, Portland's "Wine Lady," who knows where the bottles (and bodies) are buried; Bill Hatcher, Managing Director for Domaine Drouhin Oregon, a French-owned vineyard in the valley; and

Nick Peirano, owner of Nick's Italian Cafe, one of the founders of the International Pinot Noir Festival and legendary host and friend to winemakers and aficionados from around the world.

For those others who came early and continue to make significant contributions: you have not been forgotten or ignored — at least not intentionally. Acknowledging the exigencies of space and style, our intent was not to interview all of Oregon's winemakers, but to crush a history from the vintage tales of a handful of pioneers. Dick Erath has been singled out as the book's protagonist for good reason. Not only do the years of Erath's vineyard and winery fall perfectly into the history's twenty-five-year outline, but Dick is bigger than everybody else — and he owns a giant attack poodle named "Eddie."

When I first mentioned to the other guys up north that Erath would be the book's narrator, there were a few grumbling admonitions that they all be heard, that the time was right to tell "the full history of Oregon wine," and that, although Dick was a nice enough guy, it wouldn't work that way. Finally, after being assured that others would be included and the larger story told, they agreed that Dick could be an appropriate focal point. Dick, who was on their side, concurred enthusiastically.

The rest, as they say, is history.

Voyagers and Visionaries

Grapes were not indigenous to the Pacific Northwest. Legend has it that
European varieties, *vitis vinifera*, were introduced from Fort
Vancouver, in what is now Vancouver, Washington. During the mid-
nineteenth century, the fort was regional headquarters for Britain's
Hudson's Bay Company and the terminus of the Oregon Trail.

French Canadian trappers and voyagers, retired from the Hudson's
Bay Company, were probably the first to grow grapes in the Willamette
Valley. They and their Indian wives settled land southwest of Port-
land still known as "French Prairie." It is within sight of the Dundee
Hills, where Oregon's greatest concentration of vineyards is today.

It is known that grape cuttings were carried west on the Oregon
Trail. Early emigrants brought mostly sweet, juicy table grapes from
the East, but also a few European varieties. Jesse Applegate, who
led the first wagon train to Oregon in 1843, established forty acres of
table grapes, probably Sweetwaters, in the Umpqua Valley. Early
Willamette Valley settler Henderson Luellen is said to have crossed
the Plains with the first vinifera varieties in 1847.

Many of the early settlers were strict religionists with a missionary
zeal for condemning any beverages with "authority." Some vestiges
of those once-pervasive attitudes linger in Oregon, even today. However, there were enough hard-drinking pioneers to balance the
bluenoses and Bible thumpers. Some irrepressible frontier types
knocked back ample amounts of the whiskey — moonshine, "red
eye" or otherwise — that was in no short supply. Many others favored
beer, as most Oregonians still do.

Beer, whiskey, maybe a little wine, and certainly brandy were being served in Portland's first authenticated saloon as early as 1851. It was owned by Colburn Barnell, a former farmer and grocer. Coincidentally, or perhaps conveniently, Barnell was also the founder of Portland's Lone Fir Cemetery, resting place for many of the city's early pioneers. Barnell's saloon was probably supplied by William Ladd, another city father. Ladd was known to have shipped Portland's first major load of booze north from San Francisco the same year.

Portland was still a "Stumptown" clearing alongside the Willamette River in 1851. Meanwhile, San Francisco was exploding in the wake of the Gold Rush, which created great demand for beer and spirits of all kinds. Prospectors from all over the world populated the rude mining camps in the nearby Sierra Nevadas; not a few of them were sophisticated epicures with appetites for more than coffee, sowbelly and beans. Some camps, transformed overnight into booming towns or small cities, featured restaurants with accomplished chefs serving such delicacies as fresh oysters (one dollar each), caviar and the finest imported wines. Historians note that prospectors had a particular fondness for French Champagne.

As San Francisco burgeoned with thirsty, nouveau riche swells spreading gold dust over the coast, it was inevitable that a wine industry should develop in the nearby Napa Valley. From the mid-nineteenth century into the early twentieth century, immigrant winemakers from Europe's venerable grape-producing regions planted vineyards and founded the wineries still owned by well-known Napa Valley family dynasties.

Oregonians must acknowledge, if grudgingly, that Californians have been the catalyst for Oregon's wine industry. Sometime in the 1800s two German immigrants, the brothers Edward and John Von Pessl, came north from California and planted the first vinifera vineyards in Southern Oregon. The Von Pessls grew Zinfandel, Riesling, and Sauvignon. Adam Doerner, another German who visited the Von Pessls in the 1890s, obtained Sauvignon and Riesling cuttings from the Beringer Brothers in Napa Valley and returned to settle in Oregon. Doerner was a cooper skilled at making wine barrels, and it is said he also turned out a pretty good prune brandy. However, he had little luck convincing local farmers that they should include vinifera grapes among the legendary fruit crops in Oregon's warmer southern valleys.

While the Von Pessls and Doerner were struggling to establish their vineyards in the south, Frank Reuter, another German immigrant, had established a vineyard up north. His homestead was atop David Hill, later called Wine Hill, in the Willamette Valley near the town of Forest Grove. In the early 1880s, Reuter allegedly prophesied that the region would someday become the "Rhineland of America." According to local legend, his Rieslings gleaned some prestigious national awards.

In the 1960s, Charles Coury, a latter-day Willamette Valley winemaking pioneer, established a winery on the site. Now it is home to Laurel Ridge Winery, one of a handful of Oregon wineries making sparkling wines by the traditional French *méthode champenoise*.

Prohibition solidly corked Oregon's fledgling wine industry. States could ratify the Eighteenth Amendment at their own discretion, and Oregon, not surprisingly, leaped onto the water wagon in 1914, six years ahead of the nation. During nineteen years of the "Great Experiment," vinifera vines were uprooted and vineyards replanted with other fruit and nut crops. It was a disastrous setback.

Doerner, who had planted vinifera in the Umpqua Valley region near Roseburg, saved his vines and sold grape juice to local winemakers. They were allowed by law to make two hundreds gallons a year for home consumption. Following Repeal in 1933, when Oregon experienced a boom in "farmer's wineries," Doerner's son Adolph turned out some pretty good basic red wine. Most of it sold locally, and Adolph's son Ray kept the winery in operation until 1965.

By the late 1930s, state "farmer's winery" licenses could be had for twenty-five dollars. By 1938, at the peak of what was called Oregon's "wine fever," there were twenty-eight bonded wineries producing mainly fruit and berry wines, or grape "jug wines" from Concord and other American varieties. A notable exception was Louis Herboldt's winery, the first to be bonded in 1934. Herboldt had grown grapes in Europe and Palestine, and he cultivated sixty-five varieties on his Oregon property. Like Reuter, he predicted that one day Oregon wines would be among the finest in the world.

Fulfilling that prophesy would take three more decades, however.

After the fever pitch of the 1930s, Oregon's wine industry was cooled by the availability of inexpensive California wines. Not that Oregonians — or Americans generally, even in California — were gulping great amounts of what one contemporary Oregon winegrower describes as "grape juice with a buzz."

Until the late 1960s, when Americans began sipping more and better wines, Oregon winemaking was, with rare exceptions, a cottage industry. Grape wines were most often squeezed from *vitis labrusca*, native American grape varieties such as Thompsons, Concords, and Sweetwaters, which were better suited for jams, jellies and grape juice. Home-vintaged wine was produced in basements like Grandpa's, or fruit and berry wines were made and sold from small family farms.

That would all change soon, however, with a new breed of Oregon winemakers, most of them from California. They were young, educated and adventurous, and they came north to the Willamette Valley to make the "perfect" Pinot Noir. They referred to their quest, without embarrassment, as a "search for the Holy Grail."

Coming Into the Valley

THE SEARCH
FOR THE HOLY GRAIL

Arriving in the Willamette Valley, early white settlers realized the promise of their dreams: a lush "New Eden" of spectacular beauty, with a mild climate, plenty of water and a soil so rich it would return crops of biblical proportions.

After months on the Oregon Trail, trekking across seemingly endless prairies and deserts, the pioneers reached a broad green valley of deep forests and open wild meadows, a primordial parkland that accompanied the slow-turning Willamette River for more than one hundred miles. The natural environment had been left largely intact by the Native Americans who had lived here for thousands of years.

The valley had not always been so placid; its character had been shaped dramatically over vast periods of geologic time. It had been intermittently scoured by glaciers, inundated by floods and buried beneath extensive lava flows that oozed down from the volcanoes of the Cascade Range. Those cataclysms helped form some of the most suitable grape-growing soils in the world.

Today, the Willamette Valley is the largest and most important wine-growing area in Western Oregon. It nurtures not only Pinot Noir, the region's "flagship wine," but also Pinot Gris (a mutated descendant of Pinot Noir), Pinot Blanc, Riesling, Gewürtztraminer and Chardonnay. Winegrowers predict that new clones of Chardonnay will have a great future in the valley.

Other major wine-growing regions are in Southern Oregon's legendary Rogue River Valley and the "Hundred Valleys of the Umpqua,"

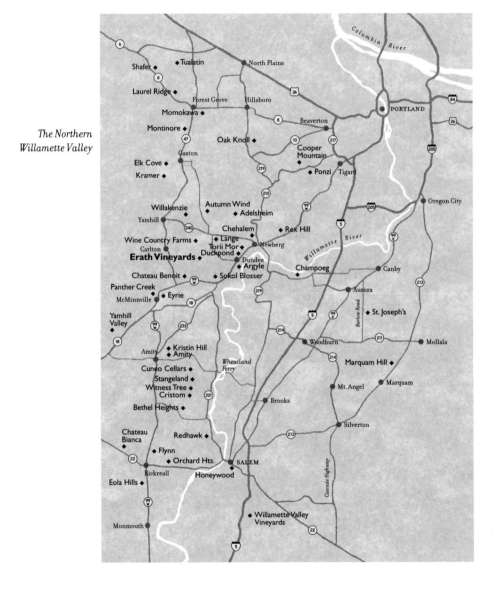

*The Northern
Willamette Valley*

tucked in and among the myriad hills surrounding the city of Roseburg. These warmer southern "microclimates" grow varieties
more common to Northern California (birthplace of almost all
Oregon vines), notably Merlot, Zinfandel and Cabernet Sauvignon.
However, varieties more at home in the Willamette Valley are
found there as well. Attempts at viticulture in the high, arid country
of Central and Eastern Oregon, where winters are colder, have not
been as successful.

Despite ongoing depredations from increased population,
industry, and the batterings of developers who keep nibbling at
Oregon's tough and innovative land-use legislation, the Willamette
Valley remains a place of soft and spectacular beauty, as well as one
of the most important agricultural regions in the land.

Most Willamette Valley vineyards and wineries are within forty
miles of Portland, Oregon's largest city. They are concentrated to
the southwest, in Yamhill County, which includes the Dundee Hills.
Looking southeast from the high-side of the Dundee Hills, the valley
spreads in a patchwork broken by low hills, stands of trees, farm
buildings and an occasional small city or town. The Willamette River
curves gently through it, and its rolling slopes are striated with tidy
rows of vines. The Cascade Mountains, some fifty miles away, form
an abrupt backdrop dominated by Mount Hood, a neat isosceles that
looks like a mountain should. "Our mother," some Indians call it.

About seventy-five miles to the West, on the other side of the
Coast Range, is the Pacific Ocean, a great rain machine whose
cool-damp infusions infiltrate the valley and determine its climate
much of the year. Summers can be surprisingly hot and dry, however, especially in this uncertain time of global warming. In winter
there are often harsh spells of ice and snow from blasts of arctic
air, called the "Gorge flow," whirling into the valley through the
Columbia River Gorge.

Although valley soils may vary within a few miles, the "Red Hills
of Dundee" contain a distinctive amalgam of soils from ancient
uplifted seabeds and clay loam weathered out of basalt from old lava
flows. Dundee's rusty, brick-red soil drains especially well, allowing it to warm quickly and promoting early vine growth. As winegrowers say, "Grapes don't like wet feet." This exceptional drainage

is also characteristic of the soils that for centuries have nurtured "the noble grape of Burgundy" in France. Red Burgundy wine is Pinot Noir by its regional European name.

In 1972, there were only a dozen wine grape growers and some two hundred acres planted in Oregon. Today there are over 120 wineries and some 475 growers, with approximately 7,500 acres under cultivation. Still, it's a drop in the vat when you consider the valley's estimated 100,000 acres of prime vineyard sites. The potential for Oregon's wine industry is underscored dramatically by the fact that, in California's Napa-Sonoma valleys and France's Burgundy region combined, only 75,000 acres of vines are under cultivation — with room for little more.

Twenty-five years ago, Oregon was virgin territory for "the boys up north," the wine pioneers who came into the valley with dreams as hopefully romantic as those of any early settler. Nearly all were Californians, highly trained professional men and former amateur winemakers who fell in love with the art and were attracted to its lifestyle. Most had taken some courses in the wine program at the University of California at Davis, where they had been discouraged from venturing into the cool, rainy north.

But they came anyway, lured by the climate, the soil, and a well-researched faith that, in the Willamette Valley, they would discover what Dick Erath calls "the Holy Grail" — an opportunity to create the finest Pinot Noir wines in the world. They began arriving in the late 1960s. By the late 1970s, they were producing Pinot Noirs that received respect and international acclaim.

At the 1979 "Olympics of the Wines of the World" in Paris, in competition with 330 wines from thirty-three of the world's wine-producing regions, a 1975 Oregon Pinot Noir from Dave Lett's The Eyrie Vineyards placed a remarkable third. The following year, before a panel of twenty judges from France, England, and America, Lett's Pinot Noir placed second in competition with the six top "foreign" Pinot Noirs from the previous year's Olympiad and Burgundies from the cellars of Robert J. Drouhin, considered the finest in France. It was the first time an American Pinot Noir had successfully competed against wines from Burgundy.

In 1983, Erath Vineyards 1980 Vintage Select Pinot Noir was

chosen as the best American Pinot Noir in the marketplace. In 1985, Erath Vineyards 1983 Vintage Select Pinot Noir won the Oregon Governor's Trophy. Richard Ponzi's Pinot Noirs were listed among "The Top 100 Most Exciting Wines" of 1990, 1993 and 1994 by *The Wine Spectator.*

Further affirmation came when the Drouhin family decided to establish vineyards and a winery, Domaine Drouhin Oregon, in the northern Willamette Valley. Over the years, there have been friendly relationships and mutual exchanges between Oregon winemakers and those in France and other parts of Europe.

For example, Dave Lett and Charles Coury both lived and studied winemaking techniques in France for extended periods of time during the 1960s. They returned convinced that the soil and climate of Alsace were comparable to those in the Willamette Valley. And in 1994, a representative of the younger generation of Oregon wine-makers, Luisa Ponzi, spent a year honing her art and her language skills in Burgundy. Luisa recently became winemaker at Ponzi Vineyards, a position that is a legacy from her father, Richard Ponzi.

The Willamette Valley offered Oregon's wine pioneers not only good soil, appropriate climate, and opportunities for a bucolic life-style, but also the wisdom of its farmers. Many of those farmers still lived on the homesteads where generations of their ancestors had tended fruit and nut orchards on the valley hillsides. Valley winemakers learned quickly that good grapes thrive where good fruit grows: in a cool, moist climate with a long growing season that allows for slow ripening; in soil that drains well; on hillsides facing southeast at best, and never north; and preferably at altitudes high enough to provide good air drainage without losing the valley's heat.

For grapes to ripen ideally, winemakers hope for warm days and cold, snappy nights. And since Mother Nature is a fickle mistress, there are prayers each year that the valley will be frost-free from the Ides of March to the middle of November.

In pursuit of their dreams, the early winemakers studied how to be farmers, and they learned their lessons well. Now, while farmers of other crops continue to thrive in the rich Willamette Valley, more and more orchards are being braided into vineyards by those who come in search of the Holy Grail.

A Saucy Mistress

WILLAMETTE VALLEY
PINOT NOIR

Although Northwest winemakers' Pinot Gris and Pinot Blanc have both
won their share of medals and renown, any "Holy Grail" found in
the Willamette Valley will undoubtedly be filled with Pinot Noir, a
wine whose seductive complexities are as addictive as an elusive lover.

Winemakers know this, and it keeps them challenged and fascinated — like golf, or fly fishing, or the search for a perfect mate. There
is always the delicious probability that a "perfect Pinot Noir" might
be impossible to attain. Here, as in the search for the Grail, the satisfaction is in the journey, not the goal.

Too philosophical, perhaps — yet appropriate for a wine squeezed
from what some consider "the heartbreak grape." Acknowledging
that Pinot Noir is not only the sexiest of wines, but also one of the most
challenging, it follows naturally that it is an "intellectual's wine."
That appellation also suits the Oregon winemakers who discuss wine's
growth and nurturing in subsequent chapters.

Professional wine critics, perhaps too saturated with their subject,
often become verbose when describing Pinot Noir's vicissitudes.
Instead of appraisals like the one attributed to Jim Maresh, who grows
grapes for Dick Erath — "Damn! This stuff is really fantastic," — they
spin rhapsodic epiphanies with words like wild, trenchant or compelling — if not haughty, or the workhorse, bold. They say, "firm on
the nose," or "finishes well," though perhaps "gaunt..."

"People should just drink the stuff and get on with it," suggests
Dick Erath, one of the Willamette Valley's oldest and leading producers of Pinot Noir. He supports this characteristically proletarian

admonishment by emphasizing that the quintessential Pinot Noir should offer "value and quality."

Erath is also capable of rhapsodizing, though. Consider this description of his 1992 Leland Vineyard Reserve Pinot Noir: "...bright ruby, with aromas of wild roses, blackberry vines, raspberry and ginger. Sumptuous, lively, cherry fruit and black pepper flavors greet the taster. Rich tannins provide a long, lingering finish, and the fine balance helps to guarantee ageability..."

Erath explains, almost reverently, "Pinot Noir is feminine — like a great woman who gets better with age."

Dave Lett concurs. "Pinot Noir is very feminine," he says. "Complex, mysterious, sensuous and compelling."

Richard Ponzi says, "The flavors are esoteric: earthy, mushroomy, gamey...You know what I mean? Like a pungent cheese. Balance is critical, because when it's off, it's really off. But," he concludes, eyes twinkling, "when it's good, it's elegant."

Bill Hatcher, Managing Director for the French firm, Domaine Drouhin Oregon, describes a good Pinot Noir as having a "good nose; it is seductive, and balance is most important. There are subtle hints of many dark-fruit flavors — blackberries, currents, plums — as well as exotic spices. It must also be earthy; the very greatest of Pinot Noirs have qualities of tobacco, tea, and leather — and," he adds whimsically, "violets. Most important, perhaps, it must evoke memories.

"André Tchelistcheff once told me that a good Pinot Noir 'must smell like your grandmother's glove box.'"

Oregon winemakers have been proving since the late 1970s just how elegant this wine can be. Their outstanding Pinot Noirs have received respect and international acclaim, pleasing even the fussy palates of the French. Hatcher of Domaine Drouhin proclaims Dave Lett's award-winning South Block 1975 Pinot Noir "the communion wine of the Oregon wine industry."

Barney Watson, Senior Instructor of Enology at Oregon State University and partner in Tyee Winery outside Corvallis, says that while Oregon Pinot Noirs will never be the same as those of France, "They can be equally as good as French Burgundy — but in various expressions." He adds, esoterically, "Burgundy will never produce as good a Pinot Noir as Oregon. And Oregon will never produce as good a Burgundy as France."

And California, with its warmer, shorter growing season, will probably never produce a Pinot Noir comparable to either Oregon's wines or those of Burgundy. However, some fine Pinot Noirs are grown in the state's cooler regions.

The importance of Pinot Noir in the Willamette Valley is apparent each summer, when the International Pinot Noir Celebration (IPNC) is held in McMinnville, the heart of the valley's wine country. Begun in 1987 by the International Pinot Noir Society formed by the early winemakers, Nick Peirano, and others, the event has been enthusiastically encouraged by the city of McMinnville. It is a sophisticated orgy of good food, great wine and socializing among hundreds of winemakers, grape growers and aficionados from around the world.

A Saucy Mistress

Willamette Valley Pinor Noir

Oregon Pinot Noirs are outstanding, and as vineyard and winery practices constantly improve, everyone predicts the best is yet to come. For those of us less concerned about whether our Oregon Pinot Noir is "cloying," "pretentious" or "tight on the nose," there are these consoling comments:

"I can tell whether a Pinot Noir is good," winemaker Dave Adelsheim says, "by the way it goes with food. I'm a cook and I love to contemplate which food might go with wine."

Rob Stuart, winemaker for Erath, is also succinct. "Oregon Pinot Noir is very good. How can you tell? If you put it in front of your nose, the next thing you know the glass is empty, and you want more. You keep coming back to it."

And grower Jim Maresh is downright blunt. "This whole wine snobbery thing is a bunch of BS, as far as I'm concerned.

"Though I must admit," he adds after a thoughtful pause, "wine is a mysterious product, and Pinot Noir is the most mysterious of all."

The True Pioneers (1961-1971)

CHASING THE DREAM

In the decade between Richard Sommer's first vintage in Southern
Oregon and David Lett's production of the first quality Pinot
Noir in the Willamette Valley, a small cadre of pioneer winemakers
committed themselves to a new industry they would nurture on
hard work and dreams. Though others soon followed, this original
handful — Richard Sommer and David Lett, Charles Coury and
Dick Erath, Richard Ponzi and David Adelsheim — shared a philosophy that distinguishes Oregon winemakers to this day.

These men were well-educated professionals who had left other
careers, from engineering to the study of German literature, to
chase their dream of producing great wine. Mostly Californians, they
felt the press of suburban sprawl and the lure of Oregon's lifestyle.
With the bravado it took to grow grapes in a challenging environment, they began with little knowledge of farming. Like all pioneers,
they shared a desire to begin new lives and careers, and to raise
their families in what some have called "the last best place."

To visit these men now, happy and at home, their success squeezed from the vineyards spread neatly around them, is to realize
that romance has been a part of it, too. After years of struggle, their
glass is filled with what began as merely a promise.

RICHARD SOMMER

Richard Sommer, the first of the "true pioneers," left his native
California in the late 1950s to establish Hillcrest Vineyard, Oregon's
oldest continuously operating vinifera winery. His rustic hillside

winery is not in the Willamette Valley, but in the Upper Valley of the Umpqua, west of Roseburg. The quiet wooden sign that proclaims its longevity says, simply,"Bonded Winery No. 44."

Sommer, a quirky and dedicated loner, planted his first vines in 1961 on the slopes of the former turkey ranch he calls "Gobbler's Nob." He now grows fifty acres of grapes that are mostly Riesling, Hillcrest's flagship wine. In smaller plots, he also plants Pinot Noir, Cabernet Sauvignon, Semillon, Sauvignon Blanc, Gerwürztraminer, Merlot, Chardonnay and Zinfandel.

Now in his late sixties, Sommer is small and wiry and has a gentle, Hobbit-like way about him. A recluse by choice, he has never married and lives in a kind of splendid isolation, far back in a remote region settled by some of Oregon's earliest pioneers. The region looks much the same as it did a century ago.

Sommer was born in San Francisco, the son of a Swiss immigrant and a nutritionist. His mother, the nutritionist, was born and raised in Ashland, in Oregon's Rogue Valley. His great-grandfather grew apples, pears "and a few grapes" there in the nineteenth century.

Because he had a desire to grow things, Sommer studied agriculture at the University of California at Davis in the 1950s. An enology course sparked his interested in grapes and wine, which led to a search for a vineyard. The good land in California was already becoming precious, so he connected with his family's past and began a careful consideration of Oregon, where the land was cheap and uncrowded and the wine industry was little more than embryonic.

Sommer studied Oregon climatological records going back some eighty years. As he recalls, "I found that the Rogue Valley was too hot and dry and would require irrigation, which I didn't want to do. Also, Medford was at fourteen thousand feet [altitude], so the season was too short. And I didn't want to go north into the Willamette Valley because of the rain and cold in winter, especially from the [Columbia River] Gorge flow."

He found his place in the Umpqua Valley, which is just south of the Willamette Valley and about one-fourth its size. The region is really a series of small interconnected hillsides and drainages, known collectively as "The Hundred Valleys of the Umpqua." Slightly drier and warmer than the Willamette Valley, it has more varied soils and about half the annual rainfall.

Sommer explains that he came to Oregon to plant Riesling, which does well at Hillcrest's 850-foot altitude. But he adds, "I've tried them all." The Umpqua region's milder climate and mellower soil allow Sommer to grow a more diverse selection of grapes than his friends in the Willamette Valley — the colleagues Sommer has labeled "the boys up north."

His first vintage was in 1963, a few years before "the boys up north" began establishing themselves on hillsides above the Willamette Valley. It was Sommer, in fact, who recognized the potential for growing Pinot Noir farther north, and he takes credit for encouraging Dick Erath to move to the Willamette Valley.

Pointing to a faded photograph taken at UC Davis in 1967, Sommer notes that he and Erath were classmates during a short course there. "Dick's become a good winemaker," he says, and adds with a shy smile, "I think I hooked him on Oregon when I showed him some photographs of my vineyard in the snow. He liked the idea that I had developed my vineyard separately, being an independent guy." Sommer also met Charles Coury and Dave Lett and says he admires them for their "pioneering spirit."

If "the boys up north" are Oregon's wine pioneers, Sommer is the mountain man who explored the wilderness and broke trail so the pioneers could follow.

CHARLES COURY

Charles Coury came to Oregon in 1965, after a careful study of winegrowing areas in and around the Willamette Valley. He finally bought an old farmstead west of Forest Grove known as "David Hill," and later "Wine Hill." He had seen the property advertised as a bank sale. He and his wife settled into the neglected hundred-year-old farmhouse that had belonged to the land's original owner, a German immigrant named Frank Reuter.

According to Reuter's two daughters, who were then in their nineties, Reuter had prophesied during the 1880s that the valley would someday be "the Rhineland of America." Apparently the prophesy held some truth. As the story goes, Reuter, who grew hops as well as grapes, won a national award for his Riesling wine. Varietal grapes from David Hill were famous at the turn of the century.

Among today's wine pioneers, everyone has something to say about
Charles Coury. He has been described variously as a curmudgeon,
irascible, stubborn, grandiose and — perhaps the unkindest cut of
all — a sometimes erratic winemaker.

Coury talks openly about his former winery, his brief partnership with Dick Erath in a nursery venture, and starting Cartwright's,
Portland's first, short-lived microbrewery. He graciously admits
the failures that sent him back to California. "I went to Oregon to
grow grapes and make wine," he says candidly, "but I left with my
tail between my legs like a beaten puppy."

Between 1970, when he produced his first vintage, and 1977, when
he left the winery and returned south, Charles Coury Vineyards
produced Pinot Noir, White Riesling, Gewürztraminer, and small
amounts of Sylvaner. He also studied various clones of Chardonnay
and their adaptation to the Willamette Valley's microclimate. Coury
believed firmly in the responsible use of modern technology in his
winery and advocated using stainless steel rather than wooden barrels, which he claimed merely "cloaked winemaking in tradition."

Now in his late sixties, Coury lives in Calistoga, California. His
former colleagues pay him grudging admiration, despite all the slings
and arrows. Most concede that without Coury's audacity the
Willamette Valley wine industry might not have developed. Despite
all his alleged faults and vociferousness, they see Coury as a fiery,
charismatic leader who simply failed to attract a following.

Coury asserts, "I was the big gun in 1965; I was a leader and talker!
Not only was I a voice for the wine industry, I was a loud voice."
But he also gives credit to those he refers to as "real pioneers," who
did the industry's groundwork.

"In the early days, there was only a handful of us who were true
pioneers — Richard Sommer, Dave Lett, Richard Ponzi, Dick Erath.
We were characters, as different from one another as fingerprints.
I remember Sommer, a very interesting fellow, telling me once that
he used to sing to his vines. I told him, 'Hell! I yell at mine.'"

A native of Southern California, Coury earned a degree in meteorology from the University of California, then became a Naval
officer during the Korean War. While stationed in Japan, he learned

to appreciate the fine French wines available in the officers' club. Intrigued and curious, he took a job after the war with a wine and spirits importer in Southern California. That job encouraged his interest in winemaking and led him to enroll at UC Davis, where he studied from 1961 to 1963.

Coury was graduated with a master of science degree in horticulture, but not without a struggle. Tapping his background in meteorology, he went to France and studied the "climate-grape connection" very thoroughly. It become the subject of his hard-won master's thesis.

"My master's thesis was a very, very clever approach to climate and grape choice," Coury explains. "I knew there were great similarities between the climates of France and Oregon, which are nearly on the same latitude. My professors argued with me, but I was right. I had an absolute climatological basis for my thesis and knew that the cool, rainy conditions in Oregon would be ideal, particularly for the Pinot Noir, Chardonnay and Riesling varieties."

Coury's thesis hinted at the future of wine growing in the Willamette Valley. He wrote: "Any variety yields its highest quality wines when grown in such a region that the maturation of the variety coincides with the end of the growing season. Or...any variety yields its highest quality vines when grown in a region whose ecological potential to mature fruit just equals the requirements of the variety, no more or no less."

In other words, like Reuter before him, Coury prophesied that Oregon had the potential to produce some pretty good wines — especially Pinot Noirs, whose quality might eventually be comparable to, or even surpass, the celebrated Burgundies of France. "Burgundy, perhaps, is not the best place to grow Pinot Noir," Coury suggested irreverently. "Perhaps the best environment may be found elsewhere.

"When a variety gains such an ideal adaptation to its district," he continued, "when it attains ecological harmony with its environment, when it produces consistently great wines, it is eulogized and the term 'noble variety' bestowed. Its fame sweeps the earth."

His professors scoffed at him. But as a meteorologist, he knew he was right. And he's convinced that his theory influenced the others who followed. With a strong remembrance of things past and his prophesies confirmed by current acclaim for Oregon Pinot Noirs, Coury says, "Listen. I talked those guys into coming to Oregon, and they proved my theories right."

DAVID LETT

Dave Lett, founder of The Eyrie Vineyards, is no meteorologist; he came to winemaking with degrees in philosophy and pre-med. But like his colleague Charles Coury, he had spent enough time in France to know which way the wind blew when he moved to the Willamette Valley in 1966.

As he anticipated, the valley's wind blew chilly and damp, much as it does in Burgundy. And as he and Coury predicted, the soil and climate of this virtually untapped northern region of Oregon were ideal for Pinot Noir.

In 1970, Lett produced the first quality Pinot Noir in the Willamette Valley — and it sold for $2.65 a bottle. In 1979, his extraordinary 1975 South Block Pinot Noir won third prize in international competition in France. Competing against Burgundy's best, it put Oregon on the world wine map. A bottle of that memorable wine now sells for as much as $4.25.

Lett, now in his late fifties, is stocky and soft-spoken. He has the rosy cheeks of a winemaker and a white-bearded countenance that has drawn comparisons to the author Ernest Hemingway. A friend from Burgundy dubbed him "Papa Pinot Noir." Smaller than Papa Hemingway, he is also less irascible than some rumors claim. In fact, Lett will tell you that his reputation as a curmudgeon comes from being brutally honest with people who hate to hear the truth.

"I suffer fools badly," he says with faint smile, but adds quickly, "Curmudgeons have a way of getting things done."

Lett is a private person whose personality is reflected in his plain, unmarked winery. A former turkey processing plant, it is located in McMinnville, which is the seat of Yamhill County and the unofficial capital of Oregon's wine country. He owns and operates forty-nine acres of vineyards: The Eyrie Vineyards, Rolling Green Farm, and Three Sisters Vineyard. Half his acreage is planted in Pinot Noir, the rest in Pinot Gris and Chardonnay. He produces some seven to ten thousand cases of wine a year.

Lett grew up on an "apple and boulder" farm in Utah and was headed for dental school when he graduated from the University of Utah in 1961. He was interviewing at dental schools in San Francisco when an impromptu drive into the Napa Valley wine country changed his life. After sniffing, sipping and allowing the good wines of California to dance across his tongue and excite his palate, he abandoned dentistry and enrolled at UC Davis. Within two years he had earned a degree in viticulture and enology.

It was at Davis that he met the volatile Charles Coury. Lett remembers, "Coury got me all fired up about Pinot Noir. That may sound strange, getting excited about a wine grape, but I was twenty-five, an age when you're supposed to get fired up."

In retrospect, those Willamette Valley pioneers look like a small cult of obsessive iconoclasts, and in a sense they were. The instructors at UC Davis all but ignored the possibility of growing wine grapes anywhere but in California. The new young winemakers, however, were stubborn individualists, inspired by the challenge of growing Pinot Noir in a tough and demanding environment.

Like Coury and Erath, Lett determined that California winemakers were not thinking too much about Pinot Noir, but about a lot of other varieties. "And in California there's less distinction. Wines of all varieties tend to taste like each other," he says.

"But not Pinot Noir. Pinot Noir is always different."

Lett spent a year in European wine regions, from Portugal to Switzerland, studying why varieties did well in particular areas, focusing especially on France and Pinot Noir.

He says, "I learned, simply, that the grape had to fit the climate. Any grape produces its most flavorful fruit when it just barely fits the growing season of the region. Climatic adaptation had developed empirically in Europe over the centuries, but it was a new idea in American viticulture."

Lett came to Oregon in 1966 and rented a house in the small Willamette Valley farming town of Silverton. "I saw the church steeple and fell in love with the place," he says.

He got a job selling textbooks and roamed the back roads of the valley looking for a vineyard. He finally settled on a slope of the Red Hills of Dundee. "I paid $450 per acre for twenty acres," he says, shaking his head in disbelief.

Lett and his wife, Diana, named the property The Eyrie Vineyards for a mated pair of red-tailed hawks that once soared over from their eyrie atop a tall fir tree. They considered the hawks a sign of good luck, which they have apparently proved to be.

Lett had been nurturing some three thousand root cuttings, primarily Pinot Noir and Chardonnay but also Pinot Gris and other varieties, acquired from UC Davis before he came to Oregon. He and Diana spent their honeymoon year, 1967, planting the first vinifera vines in the Willamette Valley since before Prohibition. Sons Jim and Jason were born in 1968 and 1969, and their first vintage was in 1970.

Lett drew attention with his high-quality Pinot Noir, and in that first vintage year he also produced wine from the first commercial crop of Pinot Gris to be grown in the United States. Pinot Gris, a white wine relative of Pinot Noir grown in many European wine regions, has since become one of Oregon's specialty grape varieties. Dave Lett remains quietly prominent as a pioneer Oregon winemaker.

"We were all close in the old days," Lett says. "Coury, Erath, Ponzi, Adelsheim and I — we shared everything. It was tough in the beginning, and lonely doing what no one else had done before. It was nice to have each other's company, and it still is. We all produce different styles of wines and have different lifestyles, but there's a bond between us. We know we've laid the foundations of the Oregon wine industry."

Why does he make wine?

Lett grins. "My son says I got hit by a 'cosmic brick.'"

RICHARD PONZI

Ponzi Vineyards, founded in 1970 by Richard Ponzi and owned and operated by the growing Ponzi family, is the Willamette Valley vineyard closest to Portland. It lies amid precious green remnants of rolling fields and farmland, just beyond the metropolitan urban growth boundary and a stone's throw away from an ominous encroachment of huge new homes.

Those "castlettes," as Ponzi calls them, are creeping toward the vineyard like some anthropomorphized menace in a Disney cartoon.

This is appropriately ironic; Ponzi, trained as an engineer, once was a designer of amusement park rides for the Disney Corporation. "I helped design the largest merry-go-round in the world," Ponzi says. "It had one hundred horses!"

Unlike his colleagues, Ponzi's route to Oregon bypassed UC Davis. His commitment to winemaking was motivated by nostalgia for his father's winemaking back in his native Detroit. His Italian family had come over from the Old Country in 1910. Like many other ethnics in those days, his father had made wine each year with grapes that arrived by train from California.

Remembering those days fondly, Ponzi says, "I wanted to recreate those good feelings and good smells in my life. And I wanted my kids in the business, to share all that I did."

Ponzi earned an engineering degree from the University of Michigan in 1959. He and his wife, Nancy, were married in 1962, the same year he moved to California and went to work for a firm that designed rides for Disney. Living in Los Gatos, Ponzi found himself longing for the old smells and feelings. He soon began making wine and carrying on the family tradition.

Intrigued with the complexities of Pinot Noir, he began asking himself why California Pinot Noirs should be so different from those produced in France. He realized that the difference might be in the climate and soil. Knowing that Oregon has about the same climate as Burgundy, he came north, took a job as an instructor at Portland Community College, and began snooping around for land.

Finally, he says, "I found just what I wanted — a place where I could raise a young family, have animals, and make wine for the small local market in and around Portland."

Today the Ponzis maintain one hundred acres of vineyards at four sites: Estate, Abetina, Madrona and Aurora. They produce seven to ten thousand cases of wine annually, divided almost evenly among Pinot Noir, Pinot Gris and Chardonnay. Recently, the Ponzis planted two exotic Italian varieties, Dolcetto and Arneis.

Ponzi planted in 1970 and had his first harvest in 1974. "I was no farmer," Ponzi explains, "but I had a drive to get back to the earth. Probably a holdover from my beatnik days, a liking for growing that I shared with Dick Erath."

By trial and error, Ponzi and his colleagues learned how to work with the climate, which they found to be dramatically different from California. By the late 1970s, when they began receiving favorable reviews, they knew for sure this was the ideal place to produce Pinot Noir.

Those early winemakers and neophyte farmers overturned assumptions by agricultural experts at Oregon State University (OSU), who claimed vinifera grapes could not survive in the Willamette Valley."The people at OSU had pulled up their test plots, which hadn't survived," Ponzi explains. "But those test vines had been planted on the valley floor and had frosted out."

"Once we started getting the press, things got going. There was real frustration in trying to get support from OSU," he adds."They were more involved in food technologies and put up a lot of resistance. Also, they had failed and didn't want anyone showing them up. And you have to remember, there is still a strong 'Prohibition concept' alive in this state."

Eventually, Ponzi and the others formed The Winegrowers Council of Oregon, which later merged with the Oregon Winegrowers' Association and contributed financial support for research at the state level. They also brought in Barney Watson, a UC Davis graduate and a winemaker, who is now senior instructor at OSU's Enology Program and advisor to Oregon winemakers.

Some early Oregon winemakers made wine from Washington State grapes as a means of survival until their vines matured, but Ponzi criticized the practice. "Buying out of state, I thought, was rather contrary to what we were here for. We kept our ideals clean from the beginning. It would be like moving to Oregon and buying grapes from California. Why? We were trying to grow good Oregon vines."

By the 1970s, when the good Oregon vines had matured to produce good Oregon grapes, Ponzi and others were producing good, even fine Oregon wines. "We homed in on quality," Ponzi says, "and we were innovators. We bucked tradition, revising labeling regulations for example. We were creating our own tradition.

"Being close to the earth makes you pretty humble," he adds. "As an engineer, I think I understand the physical world, the chemistry of wines. But there's an element of esthetics in it — an appreciation of what you create, a spiritual thing that is a combination of art and science. There are difficulties and unknowns. I'm often amazed at the results."

Reflecting on those early days, Ponzi says, "To have been a part of that wonderful experience was something. And then to see our industry grow out of it? Well, I can't help thinking we must have been made to come here. We've had to teach people why we're here and not in California, and we've done that very well."

DAVID ADELSHEIM

David Adelsheim didn't come to Oregon from California — or anywhere else, for that matter. As he quickly points out, "I'm almost a native Oregonian."

Adelsheim, who is in his early fifties and bears a slight resemblance to the actor Richard Dreyfuss, smiles and explains, "When people ask me how we got into the wine business, I say we did it for the romance. And when those same people ask where I'm from, expecting me to say we moved up from California, I tell them, "We were here. We just moved to the suburbs."

Adelsheim's family moved to Portland from Kansas City in 1954. David graduated from Lincoln High School, then studied at Berkeley and in Germany before receiving his degree in German literature from Portland State University. He and his wife, Ginny, who is an artist, began looking for property outside Portland in 1971.

"Ginny and I had spent the summer of 1969 in Europe and were intrigued with the handmade foods and wines," Adelsheim says. "We got excited about the idea of growing grapes and making wine. We read everything we could get our hands on about winemaking."

The vineyard, winery and Adelsheim's house are high on a south slope of Chehalem Mountain, within hang-gliding distance of Newberg. It's home to David, Ginny, their teenage daughter Lizzy, and ten cats. Ginny and her sister, Karinna Campbell, share a studio nearby, and their terra-cotta sculpture is evident throughout the house. Ginny also creates the winery's distinctive labels, which feature portraits of family and old friends.

The Adelsheims planted their first fifteen acres in 1972, but it was several years before the first crop. They battled weeds, mildew and rapacious birds and deer, an experience Ginny describes as "humbling." They produced their first wine in 1978, using tiny quantities of their grapes plus Merlot and Semillon purchased from Sagemoor Farms near Pasco, Washington. It wasn't until 1981 that wine from their own grapes appeared: an excellent 1979 Pinot Noir and a well-received 1979 Chardonnay.

Today, the winery produces some fourteen thousand cases a year from forty-two vineyards in two locations. Just under half is Pinot Noir, followed by Pinot Gris, then Chardonnay, and smaller amounts of Riesling, Pinot Blanc and Merlot. Recently the Adelsheims acquired new partners, Jack and Lynn Loacker, who have purchased property that will allow the winery to expand its vineyard holdings to two hundred acres. To accommodate the grapes from this additional acreage, a new, partially gravity-fed winery was built for the 1997 harvest.

Though Dick Erath refers to Adelsheim as one of the early pioneers, Adelsheim considers himself a "latecomer." When he first arrived, he quickly introduced himself to Lett, Coury, Ponzi and Erath. He's generous in his praise for the courage and dedication of that original group, and he considers Dave Lett among his closest friends. "Many stories about the early days begin with Dave Lett," he says.

Asked about his own wine preferences, he says "I can't imagine not having a Pinot Noir in my life. But what I really enjoy is getting to drink the wines of my friends."

Getting it Together

From a handful of eager beavers with more hope than experience, Oregon's pioneer winemakers have evolved into a group of skilled professionals with a worldwide reputation for creating elegant, sophisticated wines. That original handful of dedicated winemakers continues to do well. And now, along with their close colleagues, the "transitional pioneers" who came to the valley during the 1970s, they comprise an industry moving into high gear.

Among that second wave of pioneers were Bill Fuller, who founded Tualatin Vineyards with his partner Bill Malkmus in 1973; Myron Redford, who arrived in the valley in 1974 to establish Amity Vineyards; and Bill Blosser and his wife Susan Sokol, who have owned Sokol Blosser Winery since 1977.

Fuller and Redford came to Oregon with more than a little experience in the wine industry — Fuller in his native California and Redford in Washington State. Blosser, another Californian, arrived with only an appreciation of fine wines and, as he says, "a desire to grow things." All are linked to their predecessors through strong friendships built on a shared commitment to making fine Oregon wine.

And no portrait of the Oregon winemaking family, or its first quarter-century, would be complete without mention of three other important influences: Karen Hinsdale, whose enthusiasm and marketing acumen have made her an articulate and effective spokeswoman for the industry; Nick's Italian Cafe in McMinnville, the favorite gathering place of vintners and wine lovers; and the symbiotic relationship between Oregon winemakers and their French colleagues.

BILL FULLER

Bill Fuller arrived in the Willamette Valley after a long apprentice-ship in large California wineries. He had worked first for Italian Swiss Colony, and then for nine years with Louis Martini in the Napa Valley. "I may have been the first person to come here from a purely wine background," he asserts.

A balding, medium-sized man in his sixties, Fuller is confident and cheerfully loquacious. He became interested in wine in college. He taught high school chemistry for a while, but was attracted to the wine business for its people and its lifestyle. "I liked the idea that you could start with grapes and finish with wine," he says. "To me it was a 'pseudo-science,' and that appealed to my scientific nature."

Fuller had already earned degrees in chemistry, math and physics when he enrolled in the graduate program at UC Davis, on a scholar-ship obtained with the help of the Martini family. He earned a master's degree in food technology in 1965, with a major in wine-making.

His move north, to what would become a beautiful sloping vine-yard within the Coast Range foothills, followed conversations with the usual suspects: Charles Coury, whose vineyard was over the next hill, and Dave Lett, both of whom he'd met at UC Davis in the 1960s. He met Dick Erath during Erath's visit to the Louis Martini Winery in 1970 and ran into Richard Sommer the same year. Like the others, Fuller wanted to make the wines California wasn't making, and he had heard the stories that compared Oregon to France.

Fuller's old friend and partner, Bill Malkmus, was working in Somalia, Africa, when a bout of illness gave him time to read exten-sively about wine and winemaking. When he returned home to California, he began making wine in his garage. Eventually, he and Fuller talked themselves into moving north.

Fuller got started using grapes from Eastern Washington. "Dave Lett raised all kinds of hell," he says. Fuller defends himself by claiming the exigencies of survival, and points out that by 1981 wine from Tualatin Vineyards was one hundred percent estate bottled. Today, Tualatin Vineyards grows Pinot Noir, Chardonnay, Gewürz-traminer and Riesling on eighty-five of its 150 acres and produces from fifteen to sixteen thousand cases of wine a year.

Tualatin Vineyards' wines have earned their share of distinctions. In 1984, their 1980 Pinot Noir and 1981 Chardonnay won best of show at the International Wine and Spirits Competition in London. Tualatin's 1985 Pinot Noir was judged Best in State, and for two years, 1995-96, Tualatin's 1993 and 1994 vintages claimed gold medals for Best Red Wine at the Oregon State Fair.

It is typical of Fuller's full-bore advocacy of Oregon wines that Tualatin's cozy, well-appointed tasting room was the first in the state to have regular visiting hours. Fuller and his first wife, Virginia, were also instrumental in creating *Discover Oregon Wineries*, the wine country brochure that has become an invaluable tourist guide. Fuller is a past president of Oregon Winegrowers' Association (OWA) and former chairman of the Marketing Committee of the Oregon Wine Advisory Board (OWAB). During 1984-85, he helped OWAB develop a marketing plan to boost international sales of Oregon wines.

MYRON REDFORD

Myron Redford, owner of Amity Vineyards, is a tall, droll, fuzzy-bearded man in his early fifties. Raised in Seattle, Redford moved south instead of north to establish his vineyard in the Eola Hills, high above the Willamette Valley.

Of all the valley vineyard settings, Amity's remote location is among the most spectacular. Red-tail hawks ride thermals above the steep hillsides, pesky deer sneak in and out of the surrounding forest, and the view is more of Oregon than many will see in a lifetime.

Redford, who came to Oregon in 1974, confesses to being something of an anomaly. Like Dave Lett, he was born in Utah, into a family that he says was "originally Mormon." If this seems incongruous, Redford believes that wine is in his blood, and tells how one of his "great-great-uncles" had been a part owner of the once famous "Mormon winery" in Toquerville, Utah, back in the late 1880s.

Like most of the early Oregon winemakers, Redford came from another discipline. He had earned a degree in political science from Antioch College in Ohio and was considering a career in the foreign service. His life was changed one day during lunch in the University of Washington Faculty Club. It was 1970, and he was living in Seattle, where his father, playwright and writer Grant Redford, was an instructor at the University of Washington, and his mother, Ione, was head of the University reference library.

During that lunch, which Redford recalls as an "epiphanous event," he overheard two faculty members, Lloyd Woodburne and Neal Peck, talking about a winery they had started, Associated Vintners Winery (now Columbia Winery), and how they were beginning to produce vinifera wines. Redford had been making wine at home and had been interested in fine, or at least good, wines since traveling through Europe as a young man.

"To hear of someone producing vinifera wines locally was a revelation when you consider the quality of store-bought Washington wines in those days," Redford says.

To learn the business, he signed on with Associated Vintners for a three-year apprenticeship. At that time, his friends Jerry and Ann Preston owned Amity Vineyards, which they had planted in 1970. By 1974, when Redford began thinking of having his own vineyard, the Prestons wanted to sell their property. When Redford purchased Amity, the vineyard had been badly neglected.

"We had only about five acres of good vines when we started," Redford says.

Now Amity has seventy acres under cultivation. About half is Pinot Noir; the rest is divided evenly between Pinot Blanc and Riesling. The winery also buys grapes for its Dry Gewürztraminer, a specialty. Amity Vineyards has earned its share of recognition, with consistently favorable reviews as one of Oregon's top producers of Pinot Noir, Riesling and Gewürztraminer.

Amity's Pinot Noir, in particular, has won international recognition and myriad medals and awards. Wine critic Robert M. Parker described Amity's 1983 Winemaker's Reserve Pinot Noir as "one of the finest Pinot Noirs I have ever tasted." The vineyard's 1989 Winemaker's Reserve was chosen "one of the fourteen best Pinot Noirs in the world" by *Gault Millau Magazine*, after a 1993 competition among some 320 Pinot Noirs from around the world at Vinexpo in Bordeaux, France.

In 1988, Amity became the first vineyard in the United States to introduce Gamay Noir, the grape used in France to make Beaujolais. This is not the same grape, however, that is used elsewhere in

America to make wines called Gamay, Gamay Beaujolais or, in California, Napa Gamay.

Another Amity innovation is "Eco Wine" made from Oregon's first organically grown, sulfite-free Pinot Noir. The grapes are grown by Cattrall Brothers Vineyard in Amity and have been purchased by Redford since 1981.

Redford is currently a member of the Oregon Wine Advisory Board Promotion Committee and a past president of the Oregon Winegrowers Association. Over the years, he has also sharpened his skills by attending seminars and short courses at both UC Davis and Oregon State University. Committed to teaching people about Oregon wines, Redford opened the first Oregon Wine Tasting Room in 1980. It is adjacent to the Lawrence Gallery, south of McMinnville. More recently, he opened another in Pacific City.

"These are one-stop tasting rooms," he explains. "There are no other places in the state where you can taste and buy the wines produced by all my colleagues."

Redford graciously credits his colleagues. "We used to have some real pioneers, but I don't know if I am one. There were several ahead of me: Coury, Lett, Erath, Ponzi and Bill Fuller. Six if you count Richard Sommer, which you have to, of course.

"Look at Richard Sommer," he says. "Can you imagine starting out where he did, making table wine in Roseburg — a rough logging town where a carload of drunks might drive up the road to your winery at three in the morning? You have to respect him. He was the first."

BILL BLOSSER

Bill Blosser and his wife, Susan Sokol, began producing wine from their Sokol Blosser Winery in 1977, six years after planting their first vineyard on property between McMinnville and Dundee.

Blosser, a trim man in his early fifties, is an urban land-use planner who is currently a project manager for the prestigious Portland engineering firm CH2M Hill. His wife, Susan, runs the winery.

Blosser says he entered the wine business inspired, "not by a lightning strike," but by an interest lingering from his boyhood. Summer jobs on farms and nurseries in California had given him a desire to grow things. However, instead of entering the University of

California at Davis, where he had planned to study agriculture and learn how to care for the soil, he studied land-use planning at Stanford, where he learned how to preserve it.

Traveling in France during his college years, he learned French and acquired a taste for wine that was later reinforced by his father-in-law, Gustave Sokol. Blosser and Susan Sokol met at Stanford and were married in 1966. On visits to Susan's family home in Milwaukee, Wisconsin, Blosser was treated to fine wines by her father, who kept an extensive cellar. Sokol had a lot of great Burgundies, Blosser recalls. It wasn't long before Blosser was another converted pilgrim ready to search for the Holy Grail.

Working on his master's degree at the University of North Carolina, Blosser's imagination was fired by articles about the resurgence of the wine industry nationwide. "The more I read," he says, "the more convinced I became that the Willamette Valley would be a good place to grow Pinot Noir."

Blosser took a position in Portland with CH2M Hill, and he and Susan began looking around for a vineyard. A realtor suggested they look up old-timers Dick Erath and Dave Lett. They also met Charles Coury, who gave them a copy of his master's thesis from UC Davis. All the early winemakers were generous with advice and encouragement.

"It was infectious," says Blosser. "We nourished one another; we had this pioneering spirit." In retrospect, he refers to it as "pathological optimism."

Unlike earlier Oregon winemakers, who started with modest, marginally financed operations, the Blossers began in a state-of-the-art winery and an adjacent tasting building designed by the renowned Portland architect John Storrs. Blosser left CH2M Hill in 1980 to devote his energies to the winery and raising a family, and he didn't return to the firm until 1991. He and Susan lived on the property, where they raised their three children: Nik, Alex, and Alison.

During the years before their first vintage, the Blossers gained experience selling grapes to other Willamette Valley wineries. Now, Sokol Blosser produces some thirty thousand cases of wine annually from grapes grown on fifty of his 125 acres. Most is Pinot Noir, with smaller amounts of Pinot Gris, Riesling and Müller-Thurgau.

"Somehow," Blosser says, "we managed to put aside all the reasons that it wouldn't work. In retrospect, all of us were nuts. There were some bad times, but never that bad. We had this challenge, this 'Holy Grail' we were all looking for, and there was a consensus that Pinot Noir was not being grown well in the United States."

After Dave Lett's Pinot Noir received all the attention in France, Blosser recalls, "That said to us, 'This is the place!'" Back then, while most winegrowers had only modest five- and ten-acre plots, they worried about what to do with all the grapes; Blosser remembers that one of the big concerns at meetings of the OWA was, "Are we over-growing?"

"Now look at it," he says. "People are looking for grapes."

Blosser agrees that the Oregon wine industry received a "stamp of approval" when the Drouhins committed to the valley in 1988.

THE FRENCH

Bill Hatcher, Managing Director of Domaine Drouhin Oregon winery (DDO) will tell you that French winemakers bring to Oregon not only their ancient tradition, but a dedication and expertise shared by Oregon winemakers.

"There is a symbiotic relationship," Hatcher explains. "The Drouhins didn't put ten million dollars into this hillside just because it has a nice view."

To underscore his conviction that French and Oregon winemakers are inexorably joined in making the world's finest Pinot Noirs, Hatcher quotes English writer-clergyman Robert Burton (1577-1640), from *Anatomy of Melancholy*: "A dwarf standing on the shoulders of a giant may see farther than a giant himself."

Oregon is the dwarf, of course. The giant is French tradition or, more specifically, the Drouhin family, which has been producing distinguished Burgundies since the 1880s. Drouhin confidence is evident throughout the winery, which is a clean, multi-storied, well-lighted place — palatial, really — built in the French country style. It is situated not far from McMinnville, on a hillside that, Hatcher must admit, has a "ten-million-dollar view."

A young-looking man in his early forties, Hatcher is breezily sardonic. His good humor is evident in his spacious office, which is festooned with jokes and cartoons, bibelots and family photographs.

Hatcher and his wife, Debra, have been married more than twenty-five years and have two children: Harry and daughter Hadley, named after author Ernest Hemingway's first wife. Hatcher earned degrees in poetry and fine arts at the University of Michigan in Ann Arbor. A poet who refuses to publish, he confesses to having written only a line or two about grapes or wine — mandatory subject matter for classical poets — in over a decade with Drouhin.

A native of the Northwest, Hatcher was born in Seattle and finished high school in Portland. After finishing college, he did what a lot of poets do: anything but writing. He worked in a Detroit steel mill, then in a nuclear power plant. He had been working as a financial planner for a chain store in St. Louis before he dropped out and returned to the West.

He can tell you the date, September 5, 1985 (five days before his birthday), that he experienced the "epiphanal event" that moved him into the wine business. He and Debra were driving toward the Oregon Coast on their way to San Francisco when they decided to taste some wine and ended up at Dick Erath's tasting room. After a few glasses and some conversation with Dick, they were smitten.

"We thought this would be a great place to live, if you could earn a living," Hatcher recalls.

To learn the wine business, he followed advice from John Thomas, a friend who owned a small vineyard in the valley, and worked the harvest for a season. The experience taught him that he wasn't cut out to be an owner or winemaker. However, he still loved the business, and he knew the valley would be a good place to settle and raise a family.

He began working as a consultant. Meanwhile, Debra worked for Nick Peirano at Nick's Italian Cafe in McMinnville and later for Dave Lett at The Eyrie Vineyards. Fate intervened when Robert Drouhin, who had been following the development of Oregon's wine industry closely since the 1960s, hired Hatcher to consult.

"Drouhin was intrigued by what might be done in Oregon," Hatcher explains. "He had come to realize that this was the best place outside of France to grow Pinot Noir, and he hired me to help him look for a vineyard. We quickly became friends, and when the winery got underway he hired me as managing director. I've been here ever since."

DDO owns 180 acres of land, sixty-nine of which are planted in grapes. Most is Pinot Noir, but there are five acres of Chardonnay. In 1995, DDO produced thirteen thousand cases of wine, and since its first vintage it has maintained its reputation for high quality. On display in the winery are menus from the White House showing that Drouhin Pinot Noir has been served (as have other Oregon wines) at more than one state dinner.

The firm's winemaker is Veronique Boss, Robert Drouhin's daughter. Veronique is married to a winemaker, has three children, and lives in France. She comes over each year during harvest to supervise the wine bottling and racking. Hatcher learned French through correspondence courses and in conversations with Veronique, who also speaks perfect English. He lauds her skills and describes her as "one of the most extraordinary people in my life."

Affirming what others have said about winemaking, here or abroad, Hatcher says, "You cannot hide your personality when you make wine. A good wine needs grace, elegance and complexity. Grapes grow themselves; a winemaker shepherds the wine through to the winery.

"The French, you know, have no word for winemaker. They use the term *le vigneron*, or "vine grower," which emphasizes the importance placed on caring for the vines."

It is a perspective that many good Oregon winemakers share.

KAREN HINSDALE

Karen Hinsdale is often described as Portland's "Wine Lady," a position for which the primary requirement, she points out lightly, is "eating and drinking for a living." Yet she's remarkably slim for a gourmand. Her throaty voice is full of good humor as she describes how her career has both paralleled, and been a catalyst to, Oregon's wine industry.

"The fabric of my life," Hinsdale says, "has been greatly enriched by the people who grow grapes and make wine."

Before becoming a partner in the Portland public relations firm of Lane Hinsdale, which performs work for Oregon wineries, Hinsdale and her former husband, Howard Hinsdale, were partners with the late and venerable John Henny, Oregon's pioneer purveyor of fine wine.

Henny founded what was to become Henny-Hinsdale Wines, Inc. back in the 1960s and formed a partnership with the Hinsdales in 1972. The company was the first major wholesaler and promoter of Oregon wines.

Hinsdale is a native of Klamath Falls who met her husband while both were studying at the University of Oregon. They became interested in good wine while living in Washington DC, where Howard was assigned as an Army officer during the Vietnam War.

Henny was a horticulturist, who had acquired his love of fine wines while traveling abroad. His friendship with the Hinsdales blossomed when they attended a wine appreciation class he was teaching in Portland in 1971. About that time, higher-quality wines were becoming popular and more accessible on the West Coast, largely due to John Henny's efforts.

Henny had a wholesaler's license and import rights to some of Europe's finest wines, but he had not begun seeking out quality wines from the new small wineries in Oregon, or even California. Karen recalls drinking nothing but the best French wine in Henny's classes, a lot of exemplary Bordeaux and Burgundies from the great vintage years of the 1960s. "Then, you could drink well for affordable prices. So we felt, 'Why not drink the good stuff?'"

Hinsdale's first glass of extraordinary wine, she remembers, was a 1964 Drouhin Clos De La Roche, served at a dinner with friends. "We poured it and didn't know what to expect," she recalls. "What happened was, everyone became silent. That's how good it was. And they weren't wine drinkers, and we weren't all that knowledgeable at the time. But we all recognized that wine was special."

Eventually, the Hinsdales convinced Henny to explore some of the better California wines, to which they were introduced by a winemaker named Paul Draper of Ridge Vineyards. Their Oregon wine adventure began with the help of Dick Aften, who was working at a wine shop in Eugene called Of Grape and Grain.

Karen admits that Oregon wines were not that good in the 1970s. "Dick believed passionately in Oregon wine, so we hired him as a salesman. At first we were universally unimpressed with the wines, and we'd look out at the rain and wonder if anybody could do it here." But Aften won them over, and soon Henny-Hinsdale became the first wholesalers of Oregon wine.

Karen smiles and remembers, "We were learning to be wholesalers while they were learning to be winemakers. But we did want to be a part of it. After all, it was right in our own backyard."

That "backyard" was a wine frontier, and Karen describes the early winemakers appropriately as having a "circle-the-wagons" mentality. "In those days, very few people believed in them," she says. "But they stuck with it, even when people laughed and said they were crazy."

Henny-Hinsdale's first Oregon wine was made by Oregon's first pioneer winemaker, Richard Sommer, at his Hillcrest Vineyard in the Umpqua Valley. Karen describes Sommer fondly as "one of God's special people, a man with a very special spirit who's happiest in his vineyard. A lot of people made fun of him, but he produced some wonderful Rieslings."

As a witness to it all, Karen describes the industry's evolution, from learning how to grow grapes and make good wine to the challenges of marketing the stuff.

"It was a real struggle. Those early winemakers nurtured one another," she says, "and they needed each other. Some were stronger than others; our climate weeds out weaklings. And I'm sure you've heard that the wine reflects the winemaker.

"The climate was the true test for those who came early. It wasn't easy, but they stayed with it, and that commitment is reflected in the quality of their wines."

NICK'S

Anyone who visits Oregon's wine country will, at one time or another, enter Nick's Italian Cafe. It's a comfortable, dimly lighted restaurant tucked onto Third Street in McMinnville, or, as Nick says, "Right across from the Mac Theater."

Nick Peirano, owner and founder, opened Nick's in 1977, and it has been a wine country institution ever since. The restaurant entices tourists and pleases locals with its five-course meals and fine wine. Nick claims pioneer status with Oregon winemakers, and they claim Nick's as their unofficial hangout.

A quiet, balding man in his early fifties, Peirano runs a litany of names: "Coury, Erath, Fuller, Lett, Ponzi, Adelsheim, Redford—a great bunch of guys," he says. "I knew them all from the beginning. We had picnics and parties together. I still cater their birthdays and anniversaries."

Now a knowledgeable enophile, Nick says that he knew from the beginning they were making good wine. "Particularly Pinot Noir, and I started putting it in stock." He admits that his knowledge of wine was initially limited, but he explains, "I did have a deep affection for wine. My knowledge grew right along with those who were starting the Oregon wine industry. When I opened, they all came in."

Today his wine list plunks, rather than floats, onto the table. It includes thirty-five Oregon wines, along with wines from Italy and California. Dave Lett's celebrated 1975 Reserve South Block Pinot Noir leaps from the page at a celebratory $425 a bottle.

When asked what happens if any of his employees drop the stuff, Peirano grins faintly and says, "They don't."

After putting Oregon wine in stock, Nick also put stock in the wine industry. He became an original organizer of the International Pinot Noir Celebration in 1987 and served on its board for ten years. An event that now draws winemakers and visitors from around the world, the celebration began as a modest collaborative effort between the McMinnville city fathers and local winemakers to boost Yamhill County's burgeoning wine industry.

According to Nick, the city's Downtown Association had originally wanted to organize some hoopla along Main Street. The winemakers, however, wanted an upscale affair with no carnival atmosphere. It was agreed, finally, to have the celebration on the bucolic campus of nearby Linfield College in late July or early August. Attendance was limited to five hundred persons, the capacity of the College Commons' dining room.

Now, invitations are sent each year to some three thousand winemakers, enophiles and critics throughout the world, and those lucky enough to be accepted pay five hundred dollars for the three-day affair. In addition to sampling the world's best Pinot Noirs, guests savor meals prepared by some of the finest chefs in the land.

Nick explains, "It's a lot of work, but also a lot of fun. People have an opportunity to make friends from throughout the world. At first, it was seen as a way for local winemakers to show off their wares. Then someone said, 'Hey, why not have California wines?' And then, 'Why not France?' So it just grew. Now we have Pinot Noirs from all over: South Africa, Australia, New Zealand, Germany, Italy..."

A casual affair, the celebration is purposely non-competitive, and Nick explains, "We avoid that. Anyway, competition is usually something forced upon winemakers by the critics. People come here to relax and have a good time."

Nick, who learned to cook from his father, a steelworker, is from the San Francisco Bay area. He grew up not far from his friend Dick Erath, with whom he shares not only a love of wine but a passionate love of jazz. Jazz, in fact, is an underlying motif in the restaurant and plays softly in the background during mealtimes.

The restaurant seats eighty at a homey assemblage of tables and chairs, and there are no menus. Nick serves a five-course *prix fixe* dinner for twenty-nine dollars (1997), and delights in creating imaginative menus. "I have a love affair with the restaurant," he says. "I love the dailyness of it. There's something new to try almost every day."

Nick's is something of a legend among Oregonians; people from Portland and Salem, the state capital, visit throughout the year. Since McMinnville is on one of the main routes to the Oregon Coast, the place really jumps during the summer months, when hordes of tourists swarm the wine country.

"They come from all over," Nick says. "One summer a couple come in from back East, New Jersey I think. They said they had originally planned to tour France's wine country, but decided to come here instead." Cracking a big grin, he adds, "They were delighted."

Oregon or Bust

THE GRAPES OF ERATH

Dick Erath winces at that worn-out pun, "The Grapes of Erath," evoking the Depression-era travails of the hard-worn Joad family in Steinbeck's Pulitzer Prize winning novel. Blown off their Oklahoma farm during the Dustbowl, the Joads crowd into a cranky old car and head for California, the "land of milk and honey," where they are unwanted and barely survive as migrant fruit pickers.

The truth is that Erath, who has been both fruit picker and grower, can find some stories like that — stories about old cars and life's bad weather. He remembers, "My dad gave me an old Ford Falcon station wagon that I must have put eight thousand miles on, looking for places to grow grapes. That was in February, 1968. My dad thought that I had lost my mind. I almost thought so too, after that terrible wet August. I was ready to pack my suitcase and head back to California…"

He stuck it out. Today, Dick Erath surveys the Willamette Valley, just greening up in an early wet spring, from a hilltop some 750 feet up in the Dundee Hills. He claims it is the finest patch of winegrowing property in Oregon. Dick and his second wife, Joan, live here with a couple of cats and a giant black poodle named "Eddie."

Erath loves his dog, who is more like a person in a dog suit. (You want to check his tummy for a zipper.) Eddie was featured on an early Erath label, a vintage called "Chateau Plastique." It was named after the double-wide trailer that was the Erath's home and now sits across the parking lot. The wine's quality was ranked on a "poodlenoz" scale of "the more noses the better."

The Eraths' present home, with its myriad windows, rooms, decks, and alcoves, implies hard-earned success and exudes French country coziness. The high-ceilinged, spacious interior suits Erath, who is a big man, bearded and balding. He is tan from a recent stay at a new winter home near Tucson — his "drip-dry station," he calls it — where he plays golf and scrapes the Oregon moss from between his toes.

Erath is sixty-one and six-foot-four. Though not a man of extremely capacious girth, he admits to packing a few more pounds than he should. He says it's because of Rob Stuart, the young wine-maker and general manager he hired in 1994. "I'm a man of large appetites, and one of the hazards of this business is eating and drinking too much," he says, laughing and patting the stomach hidden beneath his loud Hawaiian shirt. "I used to gain weight every winter, but I could always lose twenty pounds during the harvest. But since I've got Rob doing all the hard work, well ..."

With his winter fat, Erath makes you think of a bear — an amiable, "Gentle Ben" kind of bear who would forgo honey rather than bother the bees. He walks large and with a bit of a shamble, like a man accustomed to trudging over vine-braided hillsides. Like a lot of big men, he is quiet and almost shy. It's a manner that belies the complexity and sophistication of his wines.

We're sitting at a table in the big house on the hill, spring rain outside and a tea kettle on the boil. Eddie stands by with a stuffed squirrel in his mouth, there is a plump, friendly cat on my lap, and after looking at me with mild suspicion, Dick sips his tea and says, finally, "I came to Oregon in 1968 ..."

Dick Erath moved to Oregon in February, 1968, and quickly got a ticket for having expired California plates on his car. He had visited long before; even as a boy, back in 1949, he had been impressed by all the rain coming down. Years later, as a budding winemaker with dreams of coming north, he remembered that unrelenting drizzle and wondered, "How could you grow grapes with all that rain?" He wondered again in 1968, when he was preparing his first vineyard in the Willamette Valley, and it rained eight inches during the month of August. Building a road to the site, he watched dump trucks haul in six hundred yards of rock, only to have it sink into the mud beneath their wheels.

"It was really discouraging watching that rock disappear," Dick recalls. "I knew that in California people thought Oregon was nothing but eternal rain, and if you stayed outside long enough you'd be covered with moss. With that in mind I vowed never to buy an umbrella — and I haven't to this day. It's more a matter of principle, I guess, than good sense."

It was much drier where Dick grew up, on the Oakland side of San Francisco Bay. He was the only child of Charles and Erika Erath, German immigrants who met in America, by the bandstand in Golden Gate Park. Dick's mother was from a farm near Leipzig. His father was born and raised in an old city near Stuttgart named Weinsberg. Dick grew up speaking German. Dick's father is gone; his mother, who is ninety-two, lives in Newberg, not far from Dundee.

To prove his ancestors' durability, Dick likes to tell a story about Weinsberg during the Middle Ages. Near the end of a long and desperate siege, Weinsberg's women were spared and allowed to leave the city, but with only what they could carry. "They carried out their men," he says, with a short smile.

Dick's father had been trained as a cooper in the old country. He never practiced the trade in America, even though the Eraths lived not that far from the Napa Valley wine country, where there was a demand for wooden barrels. Instead, Charles Erath worked in San Francisco for his uncle, Karl, who owned a place called The Original Coffee Shop. Dick once considered setting up a cooperage at the winery, and the elder Erath made an occasional barrel as a hobby. Jim Maresh still keeps a small, elegantly crafted example on his mantel.

San Francisco was then, as it is today, a vibrantly cosmopolitan city. As Dick's youthful stomping ground, it provided creative inspiration, as it did for so many others during the 1950s. It was the time of Beatniks, dilettantes and "Renaissance men." Dick spent most of his spare time in San Francisco and Berkeley, hanging around the local jazz scene. He repaired electrical equipment for musical groups, having noodled a bit on the piano himself, and let his mind absorb the writings of Alan Watts, the Bay area Zen guru. And now he tells the crush crew when the vintage begins, "Wine is not made by Zen alone."

After a Bay area education, Dick's engineering degree got him jobs with companies in the Bay area and eventually with Tektronix, Inc.

Dick next to the Corvette he raced as a young man in California.

The Otto Erath Küferei in Weinsberg, Germany, where Dick's grandfather made barrels for the local wine trade.

46

in Oregon. He was busy during the decade before he moved to Oregon. He served out his military obligation in the Naval Reserve, became a licensed ham radio operator, and raced Chevy Corvettes. He married his first wife, Kina, and had two sons. And he studied photography, the art that led him to winemaking.

"There was a time when I really wanted to be a photographer," Dick says. "In 1963 I spent two weeks at a landscape photography workshop, studying under the great Ansel Adams." And he is still an excellent photographer. The black-and-white prints on his walls, evocative of both Adams and Erath, are strong images even in this dark day's stark light.

Dick met Kina, who was born in Hawaii, while taking a German language refresher class in Oakland. They were married in 1961. Before they had children, they took weekend "photo junkets" throughout Northern California, and eventually into the wine country. It was on one of these trips that Dick remembers having his "first really good glass of wine."

"Kina and I were on a photo junket down in Big Sur in the early sixties. We'd stopped for dinner at The Nepenthe, a restaurant hidden high on a cliff overlooking the ocean — a beautiful spot. (It was built originally as a hideaway by actor Orson Welles, after he married Rita Hayworth.) We had steaks and a bottle of Bordeaux, a 1962 Pontet Canet. I can still remember that taste. It was incredible!"

Neither Dick nor his family drank much, though his father had been raised in one of the great wine regions of Germany. "We hardly ever had wine in the house. My dad might have a drink now and then in the evening, what he called his 'cozy time,' and I had a martini now and then when I was older, but that was about it."

In 1963, still remembering that first incredible glass of Bordeaux, Dick got permanently hooked after drinking a bottle of seven-year-old Malvisia Bianca. It came from Ruby Hill Vineyard, owned by an Italian winemaker named Ernesto Ferraro. "It was nutty and fruity, and I got this tremendous desire to grow the stuff," Dick says.

He had been fascinated with seeing things grow since he was a kid in the Cub Scouts. "We had this garden project, and I really got into it. Cub Scouts was great for stirring kids' imaginations and getting them excited about things. I became interested in electronics

*Erath's first crush
at Walnut Creek,
using an old press
acquired at an
estate sale, yielded
a single 50-gallon
barrel of Semillon
and a career change.*

because I built a crystal set in the Cubs. Later I got interested in music, in jazz, and then in photography. Winemaking played right into my background. Not only could I grow things, but as a winemaker I would be challenged as an artist and as a scientist."

"With winemaking, everything's right," he says. "It's a way of using your senses and intellect with a high degree of technical skill." Then he laughs. "It's a great occupation for generalists."

Hard bitten by the wine bug, Dick and Kina began venturing deeper into the wine country. It not only taught them about the region's fine wines, but soon had them nibbling its toothsome cheeses and breads and discovering restaurants where they learned how essential a good wine is to a fine meal. "I learned that wine is diverse, delicious, food friendly and affordable. I still love the way wine and cheese go together," Dick says. "I can't think of a meal without wine."

Eventually, Dick and Kina bought three acres in Walnut Creek, a semi-rural Bay area community not yet engulfed by suburban development. For his first vineyard, Dick cleared an old walnut orchard, horsing out the dying trees with a chain and a '53 Chevrolet. He laughs, remembering, "I tried like hell to pull the rear end out of that old Chevy, but it wouldn't budge. Those walnut trees had been in the ground a long time and were tough, but that old car was tougher."

Dick's first son, Erik, was born in Walnut Creek, in 1965. Cal was born two years later. Dick claims that he was only "playing at winemaking" then, but by the time Erik was born he was only a barrel or two short of becoming a pro. Using an old wine press he had bought at an estate sale, he put up a fifty-gallon barrel of Semillon from eight hundred pounds of grapes he had purchased from Ferraro. The quality, he admits somewhat proudly, "wasn't that bad."

"And then," Erath adds, "one thing led to another."

During the four years Dick and Kina lived at Walnut Creek, he grew some Ruby Cabernet and Zinfandel and bought wine grapes from other vineyards. In 1966, Dick bartered his photography skills for a load of grapes from his friend and mentor, Barney Fetzer, who owned a vineyard in the Redwood Valley. He gave Fetzer pictures to illustrate a brochure to sell grapes.

While still working full time as an engineer for a firm called Eldorado Electronics, Dick was moving inexorably toward his new profession as a winemaker. "I had been reading anything I could get my hands on to learn about winemaking," he said. "I was immersed; I found it fascinating. I was swept away!"

He acquired firsthand knowledge from Fetzer, Ferraro, and others skilled in the art, and he tracked down an old European winemaker named Julius Fessler after being impressed by his books on viticulture. Fessler emphasized the importance of matching grapes with appropriate soil and climate — elements that would eventually influence Dick's move north into the Willamette Valley.

Dick contacted the California Wine Institute, which supports professional growers and winemakers, and asked to be sent their newsletter. He claimed he was planning to start a winery in Walnut Creek. From the newsletter, he learned about a two-week course in winemaking offered by the University of California at Davis, which had been training winemakers through its well-established Department of Enology and Viticulture since 1908.

In 1967, Dick enrolled in his first two-week course at Davis, where he would return from time to time later. The experience changed his life. Not only did he meet some of the great names in California winemaking, such as the late André Tchelistcheff, who later became his friend and mentor, and Louis Martini. He also met or heard rumors of men from UC Davis who were heading north to create Oregon's wine industry.

In his class was the quirky loner Richard Sommer, who had graduated from UC Davis in the 1950s. Sommer, who established his Hillcrest Vineyard and winery in the Umpqua Valley west of Roseburg, is considered the first of Oregon's new winemakers. Sommer, who refers to Erath and his Willamette Valley colleagues as "the boys up north," encouraged Erath to venture up into the Willamette Valley. At that time it was a veritable terra incognita for growing varietal grapes, as far as California winemakers were concerned.

"The course at Davis was a catalyst," Dick recalls. "It opened new vistas. These were very real people, honest and sincere, and I thought to myself, 'I don't think there are a lot of jerks in this business.'"

Sommer was one of the few people at Davis even discussing the potential for developing a varietal wine industry up north. It was considered too cold, too wet — a forbidding environment. However,

one of Dick's professors, Dr. Vernon Singleton, told him about
Charles Coury and Dave Lett, graduates who had gone up into the
Willamette Valley intending to make wine.

"I thought, why not grow grapes there? They grow grapes and make
wine successfully in the colder climates of Europe. Making wine
in Oregon, I thought, would be challenging and exciting. I already
knew I'd be bored making wine in California — a place where you're
expected to make the same wines as your neighbor, and those are the
standards by which your wines are judged.

"I also got interested in growing Pinot Noir in cooler climates.
It was more flavorful and difficult than Zinfandel, for example. And
I wanted to do something different from those guys up in the Napa
Valley who, it seemed to me, were all lined up like fishermen along a
crowded trout stream."

Within a year of leaving UC Davis, Dick Erath followed his dream.
Within a few short years of his arrival in the Willamette Valley, his
dream placed him among that handful of pioneers now recognized
for making great Oregon wine.

Oregon or Bust

❦

The Grapes of Erath

From Dreamer to Dirt Farmer

ERATH IS AN
ANAGRAM OF EARTH

In France, Dick Erath would be considered LE VIGNERON, literally a
"vine grower." To the French, the care of vines is the essence of winemaking. Erath's friends would agree, telling you he is a man bound to
the earth. Dick confirms, "Great wines are made in the vineyard."

After twenty-five years in the business, Erath is one of Oregon's
oldest and leading producers of varietal wines, particularly the
valley's quintessential Pinot Noirs. He crushes the harvest from 103
acres he owns and leases, plus grapes purchased from select
Willamette Valley vineyards. Erath's first crush in 1972 produced a
minuscule 216 cases of three varieties: Pinot Noir, Gewürztraminer,
and White Riesling. In 1995, Erath Vineyards produced thirty-five
thousand cases of wine: twenty-one thousand cases of Pinot Noir and
smaller amounts of Pinot Gris, Pinot Blanc, Chardonnay and Riesling.

Locating his first vineyard was one of the most difficult tasks that
confronted Dick after he moved north. He had been hired as a
designer for Tektronix, Inc., located west of Portland in the then-small
community of Beaverton. Tektronix, known familiarly as "Tek," is a
prestigious, home-grown firm that was a harbinger of Oregon's now-
extensive electronics industry. Its growth years parallel those of
Oregon's wine industry.

Dick was interviewing at Tek in 1967 when he met Charles Coury,
one of the men he'd heard about down at UC Davis. "I drove up,
checked into a motel in Beaverton, and decided I'd call Chuck. He said
to come over and gave me directions to his vineyard. It was beyond
Forest Grove on Wine Hill, where Frank Reuter had homesteaded in

53

The unheated logger's cabin near Dundee which was the Eraths' first home in Oregon.

54

the 1880s. Reuter had apparently made some pretty good white wine there during the early part of the century.

"Coury was enthusiastic about Oregon, and so was I. We sat up until four in the morning drinking wine and talking about winemaking. His old farmhouse was a funky, run-down place. Someone had chopped a large hole in the living room floor and built a chute to drop potatoes into the cellar. But Coury didn't seem to care. He was obsessed with growing grapes and making wine, just like I was.

"When I asked how he found the place, Coury told me he saw an advertisement for a bank sale. The farm had been owned by some people whose business had been artificial cow insemination. They had died, along with a load of bull semen, in an airplane crash, and that's how he got it so cheap—only $25,000 for 165 acres. Now you'd pay that much for about five acres.

"I'll say this, Chuck Coury got me excited about winemaking. But he neglected his own winemaking, which was inconsistent, and he had a vision he couldn't fulfill."

Dick landed a job at Tek, and he, Kina, and their two young sons moved north in 1968. They lived in Beaverton for a few months, then moved into an old, abandoned logger's cabin out in the hills near Dundee, where Dick was looking for land. "It belonged to a fellow who went to the same high school I did, in Oakland," Dick explains. "He couldn't get fire insurance on the place because it was uninhabited, so I fixed it up and we moved in. It was a rent-for-labor deal between us."

He made friends with Milt Smith, a member of the flying club at Tek, and Milt flew him back and forth over the valley to scan sites for his vineyard. He wanted a hillside with good soil and an elevation of roughly three to five hundred feet, facing southeast, with good drainage and early morning sun. Searching by land, he put thousands of miles on an old Ford Falcon his father had given him.

"I used to pore over topographical maps and, at lunch time, fly over the valley. If I spotted something, then I'd go around knocking on doors." Dick smiles and shakes his head. "After all that chasing around, I finally purchased two parcels. One was a twelve-acre plot in the Eola Hills south of here, too far away to care for properly, though I still own six acres of it. The other was a forty-nine-acre parcel of the

From Dreamer to Dirt Farmer

❧

Erath is an Anagram of Earth

55

Erath augering holes for his first vineyard in the spring of 1969.

That November, the vines were damaged during a silver thaw.

56

old Dopp Family homestead on Dopp Road. When I knocked on the door, Elnora Dopp herself answered and sold me the property. Then you could buy land for five hundred dollars an acre. Not any more."

He called the property Chehalem Mountain Vineyards.

In 1968 Dick advertised in the company newsletter and began clearing the land, with the help of other Tekies. They took down old walnut trees, as he had in California, and he paid his volunteers with firewood. Eventually thirty-five of the forty-nine acres were cleared.

Then in August, Mother Nature slam-dunked the valley with eight inches of rain. When the road to the site turned into an expensive mudhole, Dick thought about packing up and moving back to California. But the rain brought some benefits. "All the pole-bean growers went out of business that summer," Dick recalls "and I bought the poles and wire for my vineyard. It was a case of one crop's failure helping another get started."

In the spring of 1969, Erath planted four acres of Pinot Noir, Riesling, and Gewürztraminer. The vines were rooted from cuttings purchased in California, from the Wente family, Dick's old friend Barney Fetzer, and Richard Sommer. They had been stored with Chuck Coury the winter before, along with cuttings from twenty-three other varieties that came from UC Davis. Dick planted an experimental block to see which varieties might make it. "In those days, without the resources of Oregon State University," he says, "we were doing our own research."

There were other problems, too. "My original plan was to move a mobile home onto the property and dig a well for water," Dick explains, looking out at the intermittent spring rain. "With all the rain in Oregon, I figured I'd dig a few feet down, and the water would just pour out. I went down two hundred feet, and what I got trickled up at about a gallon a minute. Not only was it poor quality, but that damned well cost me six hundred dollars. I thought then I'd have better luck taking my money to Vegas and playing Keno."

Then there were the twig borers. Remember all those walnut trees? "After the walnut trees were cut down," Dick recalls with a sigh, "the twig borers had no place to go, so they came over and invaded my grape vines."

That was in the fall of 1969. Then, near Thanksgiving, there was an ice storm, what Oregonians call a "silver thaw." The vines, weakened by the twig borers, snapped off under an inch-thick coating of ice.

"I almost packed my bag again. One thing I've learned about farming is that Mother Nature rolls the dice."

Like those Hemingway characters who are "destroyed but not defeated," Erath demonstrated grace under pressure. He cleaned the place up, salvaged what vines he could, and set out to learn about farming. Dick knew the valley was ideal for growing cherries, plums, and other fruit crops, and had reasoned correctly that it should be perfect for grapes, as well. "The Willamette Valley is not a monoculture like the Napa Valley," Dick explains. "Here, it's like a patchwork quilt where you can grow a variety of fruit, and I couldn't see any reason why wine grapes wouldn't grow as successfully as prunes, peaches, or cherries, given the right site."

But like all the early Oregon winemakers, filled with ambition and anxious to test his theories, Erath admits he was more a "romantic who wanted to make super wines" than a down-to-earth dirt farmer. "Back in those days, people didn't know what wine grapes were in Oregon," he says. "We had to bring them in and raise them ourselves, but we didn't know a thing about farming in Oregon."

Fortunately, Dick met two men who had been farming the valley for decades, and they became his mentors and friends. One was Grant Yergen, who lived in a small cabin near the vineyard and farmed the Dopp property. The son of an old Oregon pioneer family, Yergen had been driving a tractor since he was a teenager and remembered harvesting wheat with a combine pulled by a twenty-four-horse team.

The other was Walt Sprogis, who had farmed two thousand acres when he wasn't off steelhead fishing. "Walt basically taught me how to farm," Dick recalls. "But with Walt it was always a decision whether to farm or go fishing. Usually he went fishing, if the steelhead were running on the Trask or Wilson rivers.

"Walt knew nothing about growing grapes. But he said it was probably the same as growing hops, with vines crawling up poles and wires and everything, and it turned out in a sense he was right.

"What's sad," Dick said after a long moment, "is that both men died of cancer; both were heavy smokers. I don't know what I'd have done without them."

True to the adage, "slow start, fast finish," the experiences of 1969 ultimately proved valuable as Erath struggled to establish his vineyard and winery. He learned more about farming and about the men who became his friends and colleagues.

He was roving the valley planting Oregon Sweetwater "indicator vines" to determine the best places to establish vineyards when he met Jim Maresh. A retired Navy officer, Maresh was farming his Dundee property between daily commutes to Portland, where he worked as an analyst for Dun & Bradstreet. Maresh, who lives within barrel-rolling distance of Erath's big house, became a close friend and has grown grapes for the Erath winery for years. Dick laughs about their first meeting.

From Dreamer to Dirt Farmer

⚶

Erath is an Anagram of Earth

"Did Jim tell you about how his German shepherd nearly tore me apart? Anyway, he let me plant an indicator vine behind his barn, but I learned later his hired man had plowed it under. I think he was an old local farmer who resented us brash newcomers trying to grow grapes on good farmland.

"Still, most of those indicator vines survived. Three of the places I planted later became vineyards, including Maresh's place. Most farmers around here were pretty conservative, but Jim was willing to try something different, so we pulled up his prune trees and began planting Riesling, Pinot Noir, and later Chardonnay."

By that time Erath had made friends with Dave Lett, owner of The Eyrie Vineyards, and Ron Vuylsteke, a fellow Tek employee who established Oak Knoll Winery south of Hillsboro in 1970. He maintained contact with Charles Coury, who would later become his partner in a nursery business.

During 1969, rumors of the state's budding wine industry piqued the curiosity of the Oregon Economic Development Commission (ODEC), which was avidly encouraging new ventures. After interviews with Erath, Lett, Coury and Sommer, the commission published a brochure filled with enthusiasm for Oregon's wine industry, saying it had reached a "high level of sophistication" and predicting much of what is happening in the Willamette Valley today.

The brochure attracted the attention of Portland businessman C. Calvert "Cal" Knudsen. "Knudsen wrote letters to me, Sommer, Coury, and Lett saying he wanted to start a champagne operation,"

Dick recalls. "He had fallen in love with Champagne on a trip to France and wanted my grapes. I told him that he should grow his own; I wanted to keep my grapes for my own winery." Two years later, they began working together.

In 1970, Erath began long and lasting friendships with Richard and Nancy Ponzi and David and Ginny Adelsheim. Ponzi had just bought Ponzi Vineyards; the Adelsheims established their vineyard on the south slope of Chehalem Mountain, above Newberg, the following year.

"Ponzi is a great guy," Dick says, "a man with a real love of family and a wonderful sense of humor. I remember calling over there to introduce myself and sell him grape plants. His wife, Nancy, said he'd have to call back because he was outside chasing the foxes out of the chicken house.

"The first time the Adelsheims came over, I had the engine of my '68 BMW spread all over a blanket on the dining room table." Dick laughs. "That's the way it was in those days, all of us poor and just getting along, but all of us in love with grapes and making wine."

During a short course at UC Davis in 1970, Erath became interested in growing Merlot and stopped by the Louis Martini Winery. There he met Bill Fuller, who later came north to establish Tualatin Vineyards, just over the hill from Charles Coury.

Encouraged by the recognition and support from the OEDC, Erath, Lett, and Coury went to the Oregon State Legislature in Salem to lobby against the importation of grape vines that were not virus free. They also wanted to prevent the spread of *phylloxera*, which had destroyed the vineyards of Europe at the turn of the century and was ravaging California vineyards.

"We wanted clean material, registered root stock that was free of disease. That required that we obtain certified vines. The quarantine against phylloxera required that vines be grown in a greenhouse, in soilless media." Dick explains "We were successful. Unfortunately, some twenty years later *phylloxera* began showing up in the Dundee Hills. How it got here, we don't know. But we have lots of theories. Phylloxera is not a disease; it's a louse that feeds on the vine's roots, killing them over time."

In 1970, both Erath and Coury began to buy heat-treated vines —

"super clones" — that were registered with the state as "mother vines." Initially, neither knew they were headed in the same direction.

"Coury and I got together, began taking orders from other growers and winemakers, and formed the Erath-Coury Nursery, which we eventually located in a greenhouse out on Powell Boulevard, in East Multnomah County. We were getting orders from everybody. Ponzi was one of our customers, and so was Bill Blosser."

"Blosser was growing grape vines in his upstairs bedroom," Erath adds, chuckling. "He was using those bright 'grow lights' like they use to grow marijuana, and the light was leaking out the windows. You can imagine the cops busting in and finding grape vines. But that's how it was; nobody knew anything about growing grapes in those days."

From Dreamer to
Dirt Farmer

❧

*Erath is an
Anagram of Earth*

Eventually, the nursery partnership was dissolved. Weather and other logistical problems were part of the reason. The rest, Dick claims, was Coury's difficult personality, which had created clashes between him and the other early winemakers. Erath, who has a forgiving way about him, is the only one of the original winemakers who has visited Coury since. Coury returned to California in 1977 and, still bitter over his experiences in Oregon, is no longer involved with grapes or winemaking.

Dick says, "We were friends. He had a purpose here, and that was to prove a vision to the rest of us. What happened is what he predicted, though he wasn't able to remain a part of it. Sure, he annoyed people, but he was smart. His master's thesis was on cold-climate wine-growing, based on his experience in France. He even had trouble convincing his professors his ideas would work. They fought and argued, but he was determined and finally won. He knew what he was doing.

"You have to remember," Dick adds, "he was the first one up here after Sommer, who came in 1961, and he got me excited about winemaking. What you have to say, I guess, is that he always wanted to be a leader, but nobody wanted to follow him. And he was far-sighted, I'll give him that. You know Coury started Cartwright's, the first microbrewery in Portland. It went belly-up, but now Oregon is considered the microbrewing capital of America."

In April, 1970, Mother Nature rolled her dice once again, and the young vines Dick had planted on the Dopp Road property were hit by a late snow and frost. "The first four acres had started growing, but the young vines didn't have their roots very far down and budded out early," Erath says. "The snow and frost burned them back to the ground. I almost got the suitcase out again; but they managed to survive, and they grew well."

Dick's prospects advanced from "pretty good" to quite promising the following year, when he joined Cal Knudsen in the partnership that would become Knudsen Erath Winery.

Going All the Way

TO KNUDSEN ERATH
AND BACK AGAIN

By 1971, Dick Erath had decided to cut his connection with Tektronix to leap into the business of making wine. The catalyst was Cal Knudsen, whose request for grapes Dick had refused two years before. This time, Knudsen made Dick "an offer he couldn't refuse."

"Cal was excited about two hundred acres he had bought in the hills above Dundee and wanted someone to establish the vineyard." Dick remembers. "He wanted to start a sparkling wine operation using the traditional Champagne method, but I told him that was too much trouble and expense. Anyway, he hired me on salary and provided a shed and the equipment for a winery, and we erected a prefabricated log house on the property for me and my family. That building became our first winery, and we still use it as our tasting room."

Knudsen, now in his early seventies and retired, lives alone in Seattle. Julia, his wife of forty years, died in 1990, in a cabin above the vineyard. He remembers, "I had developed a fondness for wine, particularly sparkling wine, when Julia and I traveled in Italy and France. I was aware that Oregon could produce good still wine and felt, with our climate, we also could produce fine sparkling wine. Dave Lett introduced me to Dick; I had met Dave when he was still a salesman for a book company. Dick wanted to pull loose from Tek and start a winery, but he didn't like the idea of making champagne, which we could have made from Pinot Noir or Chardonnay. He said it was too difficult and costly — which it might have been then, just starting out."

Knudsen later became a partner with Australian vintner Brian Croser in the Argyle Winery of The Dundee Wine Company. Established in 1987, it is now one of the top sparkling wine producers in the United States. Argyle also produces Chardonnay, Dry Riesling, Pinot Gris and Pinot Noir.

The Knudsen Erath partnership was formed in 1975, three years after Erath's first vintage. Erath was the winemaker, grape grower and general manager, while Knudsen handled the business side of things. Knudsen's credentials included having been president of the Evans Products Corporation in Portland and vice-president of the sprawling Weyerhaeuser Company. He now sits on numerous boards and committees.

"I get a great deal of pleasure out of wine," Knudsen explains. "I drink it often, with food or on its own. It's very important to my lifestyle. And I was interested then, and am still, in winemaking. To me it's a sideline, not a hobby. But my interest was never in the day-to-day operations of running a vineyard or winery, though I like vineyards. I'm much better at working out financial planning and strategy — helping production by leadership, coordination and periodic review sessions, that sort of thing. I have been successful in business and know what to do if something happens."

The new venture gave Erath plenty of opportunities to test his skills — and his patience. First, the shipment of vines from California arrived late. It was July and hot, and Dick had to have water wagons brought in to keep them alive. And the site needed lots of work.

"The old farmhouse on the property had once been a house of ill-repute," Dick says, "and the vineyard site had been abandoned since it was wiped out in the Columbus Day Storm (a 1962 storm with hurricane-force winds). And then there were pea weevils that lived on the vetch we cleared away. They had stayed in the ground and were eager to chow down on the newly planted vineyards. One morning we woke up and they were all over the place. Walt Sprogis helped me get rid of those guys..."

And so on.

Despite the challenges, 216 cases of the first wine with the Erath label were produced the following year, 1972. Jim Maresh keeps a bottle from that first crush on the mantel above his fireplace. The label is of the plain-white, tongue-licked genre. Handwritten in ballpoint, it says simply, "Gewürztraminer."

Dick laughs and shakes his head. "Yeah, we had ninety cases of

*The first crush
for the Erath label
in 1972.*

*The results of that
crush: Riesling,
Gewürztraminer
and about four
barrels of Pinor Noir.*

Pinot Noir, about four barrels, and the rest was Riesling and Gewürz-traminer. And you know how I sold it? I set up a card table, and people came up the road. Later we had a wine-tasting room, and Jim Maresh's daughter, Martha, ran it for us on weekends."

Before long, however, the Erath label was leaving the Dundee Hills and traveling out into the world — at least to California and into the Northwest. In 1974, in a coals-to-Newcastle journey, Dick loaded up forty-four cases of his 1972 Pinot Noir and Riesling and headed down to a friend's wine shop in San Francisco.

"That was Jerry Draper, and he had a shop on Sutter Street. I rented a U-Haul trailer, hooked it up to my old International Scout, and loaded them up with wine. It rained on the way down, and when I got

Erath's first wines were made in the homestead basement (back left). Winery construction (foreground) began in 1972.

there the cases were pretty soggy. I remember double-parking and unloading on the street. All these guys, I don't know whether they were winos or what, were standing around watching me, like they were going to jump me or something. I guess they decided I was too big to mess with. I remember selling that batch for three dollars a bottle."

Back up north the same year, Erath's 1972 Riesling and 1972 Pinot Noir won gold medals at the first judging by the Seattle Enological Society. Two years later, Dick found a wholesaler to move his wine into the stores.

"Oregon Wine Wholesalers was started by Bill Wilkerson. He was an undertaker," Dick explains with a chuckle, "or used to be. I don't know if that's good or not for a wine dealer. I remember he was married to another undertaker's ex-wife, and they lived on a houseboat out on Hayden Island, in the Columbia River."

Dick also made friends with Bert Harris, owner of Harris Wine Cellars in Portland, one of the early outposts of serious connoisseurs. "Harris liked to call himself 'The Maestro.' He used to give wine classes, and he loved to get all rigged up in this fancy outfit and play the role. He used to ask me to sit in as technical advisor. As a result, I got to taste wines from all over the world."

In 1974, again during a conference in Washington state, Dick established his friendship with the late and legendary André Tchelistcheff, whom he'd met briefly at Davis back in 1967. Tchelistcheff had been working as a consultant to Washington winemakers.

Tchelistcheff became a frequent visitor to Dundee. Raised in pre-Revolutionary Russia and nurtured in the European tradition, he was a gracious, courtly man who cared sincerely about Dick and took a great interest in his grapes and wine. His long years of experience and expertise were respected here and abroad. Considerably impressed with the achievements of Oregon's brash young winemakers, he offered advice that was sincere and invaluable. Tchelistcheff died in April, 1994.

"He was really a sweet man who loved wine and people. His dedication to the wine industry knew no bounds," Erath says. "He'd make you think about what you were doing. He'd show you how to make sure all the pieces came together. He was a master. It was like studying with Ansel Adams and seeing how he looked at earth and light.

"Photography has to do with the eye, not luck — just like wine-making is a combination of art and technology. Though sometimes," he admits, "luck might play a part."

By 1976, Knudsen Erath was up and running, producing more and more wine while each partner was not only adding to his vineyards but buying additional grapes from local producers. A little way down the road Jim Maresh was growing grapes for Erath, as was another newcomer, Arthur Weber. Weber, a former publisher, had moved to Oregon from California, via Boston.

Asked about how he got to know Weber, Dick says, "That's a funny story. Weber came up here from California and was looking for Dave Lett. Lett's place is in McMinnville, but hard to find, so he ended up in Dundee. When he stopped at the service station to ask directions, the guy said he had promised Lett not to give them to anyone. So Weber turned up our road, Ninth Street, like everybody else. That's when he saw the 'for sale' sign on the property he has now.

"He used to come up and stay in a tent. Pretty soon his friends came with tents, and after a while there were tents all over down there. We started calling the place 'Tent City.'"

Erath was deepening his friendships in the small band of original Willamette Valley winemakers: Lett, Coury, Ponzi, Fuller, and the rest. They worked closely together, helping, advising and supporting one another as they struggled to create an industry and make better and better wine. According to Erath and the others, they shared a true feeling of being in it together. Their cooperative efforts affirmed about winemaking what the late author John Cheever said about writing: "It is not a competitive sport."

"In those early days, we had great times," Dick remembers. "We had picnics, parties, and jazz events. Our kids and wives all knew each other. You know, I loved jazz so much I named my son after Cal Tjader. We were romantics, pioneers, and we knew it. There were no feelings of spite or envy, and there was no competition. If someone had to learn how to do something, we'd all learn it together. And we had a lot to learn. None of us knew farming, and most of what we knew about winemaking was theory we had learned at UC Davis. Given Oregon's cool climate, we had a lot of unlearning to do."

"We used to get together and give awards for who whined or bitched too much. We called it our 'Tent City Awards Banquet.' We were all struggling, but we had this dream, you know." Almost wistfully, Erath adds, "And we also had this terrific sense that we were creating a new industry. It was damn hard work, but it was exciting."

By 1977, confident that Knudsen Erath wines were acquiring a solid reputation, Erath decided to take six weeks off and make a comparison check on the wines of France and Germany. When he arrived in France with bottles of his wine under his arm, Dick found the French winemakers as he had expected — reserved and a bit standoffish.

They regarded him, as they did most Americans, as a brash newcomer whose skills relied on technological innovation rather than time-proven tradition.

Dick gets a mischievous look in his eye. "You know what I did? I started passing around business cards that Tchelistcheff had given me. When they saw his name they smiled and threw their arms around me; that's how respected he was among the international wine community. They couldn't have been nicer after that."

Erath ran around tasting the foreign goods, while offering samples of his wares. Growers, winemakers and wholesalers were, for the most part, impressed with the American's Pinot Noir. "Then I met a wine merchant, Becky Wasserman," Dick says, "and she set up a tasting for the local producers. They smacked their lips and rolled their eyes; all in all they thought it was pretty good.

"And when I had tasted all that French Burgundy and found it similar to my own, I was pleased. I knew I was doing something right — that I wasn't crazy after all."

With a tentative stamp of approval from the discerning denizens of the finest wine region in France, Erath returned with a greater confidence in the future of his wines. That confidence was confirmed several years later during Dick's first meeting with French winemaker Robert Drouhin, who later purchased land for a vineyard high on a hill near McMinnville. Drouhin had gotten to know Oregon through the venerable John Henny, founding partner of Henny-Hinsdale Wines, Inc. Henny was one of the first in Portland to import fine French wines, and he had been teaching wine-appreciation classes since 1967.

Henny's first love, however, was horticulture, a field in which he had achieved international recognition. He was the founder of the American Rhododendron Society, as well as a member of the Royal Horticultural Society in Britain, and it was his flower business that led him to a new career. While in England to buy rhododendrons, he sampled some of the great wines of Europe and came back excited about bringing them to Oregon.

So when Drouhin came up the road to the Knudsen Erath winery for his first meeting with Dick, he was packing a bottle of his family's famed Burgundy that he'd picked up from Henny. Dick says,

"Drouhin came into the tasting room, introduced himself, then went back to his car and got his wine. I poured him a glass of mine, then tasted his. We agreed that they were similar, which pleased us both.

"Then I laughed and told him, 'You know, Robert, the day will come when I'm visiting in Burgundy, and I'll run down to the local distributor and get a bottle of my wine.' He got a big kick out of that. Drouhin had been visiting with winemakers throughout the valley, and I do think he was impressed. And I honestly think it was after that trip he decided to come to the valley."

During the late 1970s and early 1980s, Knudsen Erath wines improved even more, gaining greater attention locally and receiving accolades nationwide. Other Willamette Valley Pinot Noirs, like Dave Lett's superb 1975 South Block which had competed so well in France, were also receiving recognition. Dick likes to emphasize that "Pinot Noir had never reached perfection outside of France until the Oregon bottlings of the mid-70s."

"Our vineyards were kind of running on five cylinders until 1980," Dick explains. "We were able to boost our production to ten thousand cases. What really put us on the map was a great review in *Wine & Spirits* magazine in January, 1984. Then we were on our way." During that time of growth and prosperity, Knudsen Erath recorded only one aberration. It was a successful one, it turned out, so Dick laughs about it now.

"In 1984 we had an unusually cold fall. It rained and rained, and it was about ten degrees cooler than normal, with no sun breaks. We were having November weather in October, and when I called the weather bureau it was bad news for the rest of the season. The Pinot Noir didn't ripen properly; it was only about 16.5 percent sugar content.

"We went ahead and crushed the grapes into what we called Pinot Noir Blanc, a pale pink wine. Later we added a Riesling Sweet Reserve and called it 'Coastal Mist.' It was our 'Oregon hot tub wine.' And you know what? It sold like crazy, especially among the yuppies."

While his wine business was prospering, Dick's personal life was floundering. Many of the Oregon winemakers talk about the strain placed on their marriages by those early years of struggle and near-obsession with success. Dick and his first wife, Kina, separated in 1984. They divorced in 1987, about the same time Erath was concluding his partnership with Cal Knudsen.

By then the vineyard was producing some thirty-five thousand cases of wine. That's about as much as it produced last year (1996) and, according to Dick, a comfortable amount for the size of his winery. The winery's continued success provided Erath with the financial resources to buy out Cal Knudsen in 1988. Dick kept the winery, inventory, buildings and equipment, and obtained a long-term lease on the land they stand on.

It's not quite clear what happened between the men, though Dick occasionally emits some low growls hinting at past disharmony. Knudsen claims he instigated the breakup. "It was time to split. I initiated the dissolution, and he had the right to buy me out," he says, adding graciously, "and actually, it was Dick's winery."

Then he hints at the real reason behind the split, which perhaps, over time, rose slowly to the surface like the bubbles in a glass of Champagne. "Dick had done all the work, and he was always trying hard to produce a quality wine at the lowest affordable price, while I had always wanted to develop my own winery to produce quality sparkling wine. Now I've got Argyle. I'm also involved with a vineyard in Central Washington, but Argyle is most important to me right now."

Dick's lingering irritation may have to do with the fact that while splitting from Knudsen he was also involved in contesting a bitter, lengthy, expensive divorce. And it's a sad irony that Knudsen's wife died suddenly in 1990, and Kina Erath died four years later, so that neither had a chance to enjoy the blossoming of the industry they'd helped start.

"Essentially, I was involved in two divorces — one from my wife and the other from Cal Knudsen. But," Dick relents, "he's a nice guy, and I have no animosity toward him. He was just more of a businessman, while I'm more into the business of making wine."

Knudsen has no bitterness. "I'm very high on Dick," he comments. "He's a totally focused individual, someone who is able to completely concentrate on what he thinks is important. He's not perfect, but who is? We had a lot of good years together, and what he's done is an incredible accomplishment."

The Holy Grail

It's spring, and from his big house on the hill Dick Erath can look deep
into the valley and over the surrounding Dundee Hills. The red
earth supports vines that should show new green any day now. Far
off over the valley there are thunder clouds, gray, white and as various as those in an El Greco painting, and rain falls discriminately
through rays of God light.

Eddie the poodle is a curly dark presence, and the cats doze somewhere. Dick's second wife, Joan, will be home soon. Joan is a lively,
loquacious New Jersey native who was working for Henny-Hinsdale
Wines, Inc., when she and Dick met at a Christmas party in 1986.
They were married in 1990. Though Dick is quiet about it, many of
his old friends give Joan considerable credit for his recent success.
She's "the best thing that's happened to him" they say, because she's
responsible for good-naturedly "getting on his case" now and then.
Dick doesn't talk too much about Joan, being a big, shy guy, but he lets
out enough to confirm that he loves and respects her.

Joan was aware of Dick's shyness when they first met. It was part of
his appeal, as was the fact that he was a winemaker. It all fit. "Dick's
good company," she says. "Smart, entertaining and has a terrific sense
of humor. Droll, you know?"

Joan's first marriage ended in 1978, three years after she came out
to Oregon and began working with Henny-Hinsdale. Her three
daughters, Nancy, Judy and Maggie, all live in Portland. Her young
grandsons, Jack and Alex, are frequent guests.

"When I first met Dick," she says, "he was pretty stressed. But I

Joan and Dick Erath

straightened him out," she adds with a laugh. Since they married, Dick has been learning how to relax. In addition to the vineyard, they have homes in Tucson and at Black Butte in Central Oregon. Dick has taken up golf.

Joan had a long interest in wine before they met. "I started drinking premium wine back in the 1970s," she says, " and I enjoy it. I think wine relaxes people. It adds to social occasions and enhances food, you know. I thought living with a winemaker would be a wonderful way to live."

Joan loves "being out here on the farm." After they were married, she managed a lot of the winery operation. "I got the tasting room up and running," she says, "but I don't do as much now."

Looking down into the valley, where there is a layer of summer haze, Joan says quietly, "You know how you start life with goals, things you'd like to do? Well, it's all reality now. Life is good."

Down below on the hillside, adjacent to the greenhouse where Dick plans to build a new and much larger winery someday, a Mexican crew works quietly, pruning the vines in anticipation of buds expected to pop any day now. This is what a lot of men Erath's age would call "happy time," a well-deserved reward after twenty-five years of intense dedication to his vineyards, his wine and an industry set to pop like the buds on the vines outside. It's the time of dreams and reflections.

Dick looks with contentment on his acreage and says he's glad he came north. "Here, we're still evolving, developing our own styles. It's exciting because Oregon is not an easy place to make wine. And the more you know, the more you don't know."

Which brings us back to that winemaker's Holy Grail. Pinot Noir represents seventy percent of Erath's estate-bottled wine, Erath produces four grades of Pinot Noir: Regular, Vintage Select, Blended Reserve, and Single Vineyard Select Reserve. All, he says, are known for their "fidelity to the grape" and their value. It is Dick's firm belief that "anyone can spend fifty dollars and get a good wine. The trick is to produce great Pinots at all prices."

In addition to Pinot Noir, Erath produces some fine Cabernet Sauvignon, Gamay, Chardonnay, Dry Riesling, Dry Gewürztraminer, Pinot Blanc and Pinot Gris (both of which took medals at the Los

Angeles County Fair), Sauvignon Blanc, White Riesling, and Late Harvest White Riesling.

Dick grows or buys, as Richard Ponzi says, "all the Pinot Noir he can get." He also grows lesser amounts of Pinot Gris and Pinot Blanc. Erath feels both are true "Oregon giants," destined to eventually share attention with Chardonnay as the big three white wines, locally and nationally.

It was Dave Lett who made Oregon's first Pinot Gris in the 1970s. Ponzi Vineyards and David Adelsheim followed. Today more than thirty Oregon wineries are making Pinot Gris. Most are in Yamhill County. Virtually all Yamhill County vineyards produce Pinot Noir.

"The advantage of Pinot Gris," Dick explains, " is that it needs no oak extract and can be drunk six months after vintage. It's a medium-bodied wine with depth and complexity. Its color ranges from light golden yellow to copper-pink, and it has aromas reminiscent of apples, pears and sometimes melon. It goes very well with Northwest seafood, particularly salmon."

Other varieties planted include White Riesling, Chardonnay, Gamay, and, more recently, two rather exotic Italian varieties, Dolcetto and Arneis. The latter is a grape grown by the ancient Romans — and by Richard Ponzi, who provided Erath with cuttings.

Asked how many grape varieties there are, Dick says, "Probably five hundred." Then he hesitates. "Maybe even a thousand. I don't think anybody knows for sure, because of the different names for so many of the same varieties in countries around the world."

From this perch 750 feet above the valley, Dick can see his winery and Knudsen's vineyards to the right, Jim Maresh's eighty-year-old bungalow and vineyards straight down the hill, and Arthur Weber's old yellow farmhouse and vineyards to the left, all close and cozy.

"It has taken me twenty-five years to become a success in this business," Dick says without smugness, but with a trace of pride. "And the amazing thing is, since 1972 I've really had only two bad vintages, in 1977 and 1984, when it rained heavily at harvest." In recent years, his best vintage years overall have been 1985, 1991, and 1994. In the years between, he re-established his Erath Vineyards label with the release of his 1992 Leland Vineyard Reserve Pinot Noir and 1993 Reserve Chardonnay.

"When I came up here, my original vision was to match the right grapes with the region and catch a 'window in time,' so to speak. That means when the climate is working with you. At first you figure you might have a 'bust year' one out of seven, but that hasn't happened.

"The vines must struggle," he says, echoing Richard Sommer. "To have intensity and elegance, good fruit ripens over the longest possible growing cycle, like the one we have here and in parts of Europe. Pinot Noir, for example, is not happy with big swings in daily temperature; it doesn't want to be at the end of a yo-yo.

"The soil must be right, too. As the French say: red wines on red soil, whites on white. In the Willamette Valley, red wine grapes do best in areas of well-drained, iron-rich soil, while whites thrive in the lighter soils. In the past twenty-five years we've learned a lot about growing grapes in the right places."

In a good year, Pinot Noir is harvested from the beginning of October through mid-November, before the first frost. After cold soaking, Erath's Pinot Noir is fermented in closed-top stainless steel tanks at temperatures between eighty-seven and ninety-two degrees. Following about a week of fermentation, the wine undergoes a period of maceration (soaking with the skins) that lasts from five to six days, then is aged in sixty-gallon French oak barrels for up to a year before bottling.

Chardonnay is both barrel- and tank-fermented. Chardonnay gains its "crisp citrus flavors" in closed-top stainless steel fermenters. French oak barrels give it complexity and balance. Barreled wine averages seven to ten months aging before being blended and bottled. Pinot Gris, which is harvested in late-September to mid-October, is fermented in stainless steel at a cool fifty-two degrees. Two months of barrel aging follow in older, neutral oak to "round out the wine," which is then bottled and released in early spring.

Considering the fine quality of his wine, Dick Erath is less than pedantic in his winemaking philosophy. "Wine is liquid food," he says. "We're not trying to reinvent the wheel every time we make wine. In the early years it was 'earn while you learn.' What we learned was that winemaking requires having the right grapes at the right place, then not making a left-hand turn in the middle of the freeway. In other words, don't screw up!"

The Holy Grail

*It's Around
Here Someplace*

Driving out to Dick's original vineyard on Dopp Road, on a sunny spring day with a blossomed drowsiness about it, I ask him a corny old question: What does he enjoy most as a winemaker?

Without missing a curve in the road, Erath says,"The best time is during harvest. The hardest part of the whole thing is knowing when to pick the grapes. That's the most important thing of all, since each variety has its own time and flavor curve. After that, knowing everything's all right, there's the satisfaction of having done something well."

The business of winemaking, he explains, "is a balance of everything: technology, art, and science. You have to create and maintain your customers by making the best wine you can from the best fruit, remembering all the while that the wine reflects the personality of the winemaker."

After having been his own winemaker since 1972, Dick decided to ease off in 1994. He hired a new but experienced young man, Rob Stuart, as his winemaker and general manager. Stuart's personality has proved appropriate for Erath wine, and he and his wife, Maria, have become like members of the family.

"Rob's like a surrogate son," Dick says kindly, without mentioning that neither of his sons have any serious interest in the wine business. "I did most of the work until he came along. I never felt I had to compete with anyone but myself, and I've always asked myself, 'How can I make it better?' I was quickly impressed with Rob, who feels the way I do. He has a fire in his belly, and he's committed to doing the job and doing it right the first time."

ROB STUART

Rob Stuart, who is forty-three and lives in McMinnville, is one of those medium-sized, baby-faced guys with all their hair who can pass for thirty in dim light. He and Maria met in 1990 at the International Pinot Noir Celebration, of which she is now executive director. They were married two years later.

Like a lot of people, Stuart came to Oregon's wine industry almost serendipitously, though not without some hard apprenticeship. Stuart is originally from Buffalo, New York, and studied biochemistry at Rensselaer Polytechnic Institute.

*Rob Stuart,
winemaker and
general manager
of Erath Vine-
yards, with Dick
Erath.*

"Basically, I didn't like wine," he confesses. Then, at seventeen, while visiting his brother Joe in Britain during his first trip abroad, he was roaming the countryside in Norfolk. "I remember the colors," he says, "vivid greens and blues ..." Passing a vineyard, he encountered a middle-aged man standing by the road, with a bottle of wine and some glasses on a tray.

"Hey!" the man said in a thick Slavic accent, "You vant some bloody Bollinger?"

Stuart grins, "It was like no wine I'd tasted before."

The man was Jezda Miljkovic, a Serbian immigrant in his early fifties who was a master of wine. He had been an engineer and a coal miner, and had somehow made himself a millionaire. So he was growing grapes and making wine.

"Basically," Stuart recalls, "Jezda was the guy who got me turned on to wine. His family had grown grapes on land they owned in Serbia, but the Nazis invaded during World War II and took it away. The Russians took it from the Nazis and gave it to the Yugoslavian Communists, Jezda fighting them all the way. Finally Jezda emigrated to Norfolk. His degrees were in engineering, not enology, yet he knew everything about wines from all over the world. We became friends, and he invited me back."

Stuart returned to England in 1976 and stayed for four months, working in Miljkovic's twenty-acre vineyard. "It was that experience that got me hooked. From Jezda I learned that wine was not something you just slam down; not just another alcoholic beverage. Winemaking, I learned, was an art as well as a science, and part of the 'joy of life.' I grew up. I learned about a whole new part of life I hadn't experienced."

Returning to the United States to put his recently completed college degree to work, Rob was still heady with wine fumes. Unable to find a job in Buffalo, he headed south, as he says, "in the blizzard of '76." He went first to Austin, Texas, then on to Houston, where he found a position as a research technician at Baylor University.

"I was working there with Liliana, a technician from Chile, who told me all about the Chilean wine culture. They grow a lot of grapes and make some fine wine in Chile, and Liliana told me about a culture of people she said were 'high on the wine thing.' From her I learned that you could make wine and get paid for it. I researched it for awhile, but I didn't know where to go with it. But by now I knew I wanted to do the whole thing, grow grapes and make wine."

Stuart left Texas and headed west, where he heard about the wine studies program at UC Davis. There he met Dr. Ann Noble, a professor of enology, who first asked if he had a lot of money (a prerequisite for ambitious wine ventures), then encouraged him to take some basic courses and start working in wineries.

"She was like a mother hen," Stuart recalls fondly. "She wished me good luck, and I moved to St. Helena and got a job on the bottling line at the Hanns Kornell winery, which was producing Champagne in the Napa Valley." Stuart stayed on for six months at the winery, cleaning tanks, blending, doing general cellar work and learning some tricks of the trade, "including freezing my hands off."

Finally he got a call from his brother Joe, who was working for a contractor who also had a vineyard and winery up in Oregon's Rogue Valley. "The guy's name was Frank Wisnovsky," Stuart recalls, "a hell of a nice guy. Frank got into the wine business — Valley View Vineyard, it was called — in the early 1970s, because he'd heard the valley was a good place to grow Cabernet."

Wisnovsky was, coincidentally, one of the first customers of the Erath-Coury Nursery. His first release was in 1976. In the summer of 1980 he was doing so well he sold his construction company and had plans to take his wine out on the road and sell it. Unfortunately, he died in a diving accident before he could see his plans to fruition.

Stuart was at Valley View from 1981 to 1985, at first cleaning tanks and doing cellar work, then taking on other jobs, including reviving a twenty-two-acre vineyard that had suffered terrible neglect. "When I arrived the vineyard was producing eleven tons of grapes, and by 1982 we were producing sixty-six tons. That was my boot camp," Stuart says. "I was up at all hours, and I was working harder than I ever had. But I knew it was for a reason; that it was important to know how to grow grapes if I was going to make wine."

Eventually, Rob moved into marketing at Valley View, then he began building relationships with others in the industry. He was an original member of the Southern Oregon Chapter of the Oregon Winegrowers' Association in the late 1970s. He made a number of contacts "through the grapevine," and in 1985 was offered a job as winemaker at Staton Hills Vineyards near Yakima, the heart of Eastern Washington's famed fruit-growing region.

"I planned to stay there only five years, but I ended up being there almost ten. I'd probably still be there," Stuart says, "if I hadn't met Maria. I took her to Yakima, which was a pretty tough town, and after one look around she said, 'Let's get out of here!'"

Maria, who has a degree in journalism from Valparaiso University in Indiana, had some background in wine before moving to Oregon in 1991. She had worked in a Chicago restaurant, Jean Claude's, as well as for a wine distributor in the windy city. "I'd heard about what was going on in Oregon," she says, "and I moved to Portland intending to get some kind of job in the wine industry." She took a job as a rep for Hinman Winery.

Stuart explains, "I wanted to work in the wine industry, but after living in Yakima I wanted to live within an hour of Portland. I knew that to get a start in Oregon I might have to work cheaply and then 'prove up.' But I felt confident, since I already had a track record."

Stuart first met Dick Erath at an Oregon Winegrowers Association meeting in 1982. "There was a general meeting and Dick came in late. Just walked into the room with a big grin and his bib overalls, and everybody sort of stopped because he imparted a kind of warmth. I remember that."

Later, the owners of Bethel Heights Winery outside of Salem — Terry Casteel, Marilyn Webb, Ted Casteel, and Pat Dudley — introduced them. "I'd heard stories about Dick. People had told me, as they say about horses, 'He'll work you hard and lay you down wet.' But Terry Casteel said, 'Listen, if anybody could work for Erath, you could.'" Stuart admits he liked the challenge.

The way Stuart tells it, he and Dick "sort of researched each other, and it was an experiment on both sides. I remember the day Maria and I went to his house to meet with Dick for the first time. He came in with a goose over his shoulder and said, 'We're going to have this for dinner.' We did, too; he cooked it right there in the fireplace.

"We got along, and it looked like the sort of work I wanted, but I had some reservations. He wanted an enologist who would do what he was told, and he also said I was making more than he could afford.

Dick has a reputation for being cautious with money — unless you challenge him and prove what you can do. I said that I'd take the job, but it was a twenty-seven percent pay cut. He said, 'Hey! If you're so expensive you must be good.'

"Dick's wife, Joan, was fifty percent responsible for the decision to hire me, which is reassuring in a family-owned business. We feel like we've found a home, and we're very comfortable with Dick and Joan."

Stuart has nothing but respect for Erath. "Dick worked really hard to put that winery where it is today. He's incredibly fair, but he can be just as difficult to communicate with as I am. That's why we communicate so well."

What appeals to Stuart is Dick's philosophy that winemaking shouldn't be about making money, but about making good, affordable wine available to the common man. "There's a lot of ego involved in winemaking," Stuart concedes, "but it's also like having two personalities. Everyone wants to have the best wine — the small, boutique, hard-to-get wine for the so-called 'elite.' Yet at the same time they want everybody consuming wine as part of their everyday life.

"There are two kinds of competitors," he explains, "One wants to be more important than Gallo in producing jug wines; the other wants to make a nice wine that sells for fifty dollars. Dick's skill is making a good quality wine without cutting corners, and he's the best at it.

"Anyway," Stuart continues, "price often influences the perception of quality; it's all 'smoke and mirrors,' like Hollywood. Oregon Pinot Noir is generally very good. Spending forty dollars on an Oregon Pinot Noir is like spending eighty dollars on a Pinot from somewhere else."

Since grapes are the key to good winemaking, Stuart, like his boss, stresses the importance of topography and the value of preserving the valley's hillsides for Oregon's growing wine industry. "On these hillsides, there's always a chess game going on between developers and grape growers. The hills are limited and there's only so much land. So the question is always: Should it be houses or grapes? But the cost of grapes is going up now, and you can estimate 300 to 450 tons from one hundred acres. That keeps new vineyards coming in."

As Erath's winemaker, Stuart enjoys his job. But as general manager, he confesses he'd rather be winemaking. "I enjoy the winemaking and some of the marketing, but not necessarily the day-to-day managment of people and their tasks. The further I get from winemaking, the less I'm motivated. But it's fine right now, and Dick's a good guy and good boss.

"You know, Dick's nickname is 'bon vivant' because he likes life and what life has to offer. That's what attracts and holds a lot of us: the clean air, the exercise and being out of doors; most of all the wine and good food, talking and sharing good feelings. That's what keeps us in the vineyard."

From the Vine Came the Grape

GROWERS JIM MARESH
& ARTHUR WEBER

JIM MARESH

Outside, the rain is the Oregon kind — steady, drizzly, and viscous. The
Dundee Hills have faded into mottled impressions of gray and
green. In the living room of Jim and Loie Maresh's eighty-year-old
bungalow farmhouse, it's cozy and warm. Rex, a gentle Labrador
retriever with "please be nice to me" eyes, rests his big head on his
paws and watches as Loie lays out a plate of homemade muffins for
Jim and me.

Maresh (pronounced "marsh") is seventy-one, the same age as
Loie, and he has a lot to talk about. He begins by explaining the oil
painting over the fireplace. It's a landscape of rolling hills and vineyards painted by Bob Hudson, a winemaker who traded it to Maresh
for a ton of Pinot Noir.

"I probably got the better deal," Maresh says merrily. "He was a good
winemaker but a much better painter."

Marsh himself is a farmer, not a winemaker. When he began growing grapes for Dick Erath back in 1969, it was only some Riesling
and Pinot Noir. Now he points out the window to some fifty acres
planted in Pinot Noir, Chardonnay, White Riesling, Pinot Gris and
Sauvignon Blanc.

The vineyards are downhill from the bungalow, across Worden Hill
Road (Ninth Street), which runs up from Dundee, through Maresh's
property, then past Arthur Weber's house and on to the Erath Winery.
Between the bungalow and the road is Maresh's "Little Red Barn,"
the storage and tasting room for his own Maresh Red Hills Vineyard

label. Maresh has what is known in Oregon as a "farmer's license," allowing him to sell "custom made" wines produced from his grapes. His wine is bottled by Erath, Argyle, and Rex Hill vineyards.

As Maresh explains, "These grapes are grown and bottled separately and can only be sold in my tasting room. I had planned to have my own winery originally, but this way I have all the privileges of a winery without all the hassle."

Maresh found his way up Worden Hill road some years before Erath, naively looking, he says, "for just a view lot in the country. We had five kids, we had already moved five times in California and Nevada, and I was working as an analyst for Dun & Bradstreet in Portland." He was also finishing a career as a commander in the Naval Reserve.

Jim Maresh

Before very long, weary of commuting between Dundee and Portland, he left his job, retired from the Reserve, and became a full-time farmer.

"At one time we were farming all you can see out the window." he says. "We began buying and leasing land from farmers who were retiring, and before long I had two hundred acres of filberts, walnuts, prunes and cherries. Our goal was to give all five kids a college education, and we hoped someday they'd come back to the farm."

Jim and Loie met as students at the University of Wisconsin and married in 1948. They have three sons, Jim, David, and Joe, and two daughters, Martha and Marygrace. The Mareshs first came to Portland on their honeymoon; Jim had earned their four-hundred-dollar train fare working as a hod carrier. Before they returned, Jim served in the Korean War and worked in California and Nevada.

His meeting with Dick Erath, whom he describes as a man of "guts and cheer," was fortuitous for both men.

"Before we started growing grapes, we'd been farming various crops with limited success," Maresh says. "Then one day Dick Erath showed up driving an old, beat-up BMW. He was a big guy with a beard and had something under his arm. He said, 'I'm Dick Erath and I've been looking all over the country for a good viticulture site. Are you interested in trying a new crop?'"

He laughs. "We were sitting on five hundred tons of unsold prunes, and the price of prunes had dropped to forty dollars a ton. I threw my arms around him and said, 'Hey! I'm interested. What have you got in mind?' I told him we'd tried black caps, walnuts, cherries... everything. People come around now and say, 'You must have gotten into the grape growing business because of the romance. I say, 'Hell, no! I was desperate!'"

Maresh knew the Dundee Hills had been a prime fruit area since the late 1880s, when it was settled by farmers who named it after a region of their native Scotland. "What you want for grapes," he says, "is a slope with good southern exposure, frost free, and with good, well-drained soil; here we have clay loam and decayed basalt, which is perfect." So it was good fortune when big Dick Erath asked him to plant an "indicator vine" on his property to take a reading on its potential.

"Well, I planted that vine," Maresh remembers, "out behind the farm manager's house, over there next to the barn. But the farm manager wiped it out, either accidentally or on purpose, and Dick came up here steaming mad. Kina told me later that he came home yelling about 'those Oregon farmers! They don't deserve to grow wine grapes!'"

Maresh had confidence in Dick and was quick to realize that while Erath was not an experienced farmer, he came to winemaking with the discipline and dedication of a professional.

"They all did, all those early guys," Maresh says. "Dave Lett, Chuck Coury, Ponzi…They were professionals who had given up other careers to come up here and make wine. And they were serious about it. When Dick came up here with his maps, books and everything, we said, 'Okay, let's go. What do you need?' We were ready for anything. But then, we had taken a lot of gambles. We gambled on coming out to Oregon in the first place, and then having five kids, and buying this place…" He laughs, thinking of it.

Dick had cuttings from the Wente family in California and told Maresh they would need a greenhouse to get them started. "Well, that put us in a bind. We needed about fourteen hundred dollars, so I went to see our banker. He just looked at me and said flat out, 'You can't grow grapes in Oregon.' That's the way it was in those days. So, 'what the hell,' I thought, and I put the greenhouse under our fund for diesel oil. We called it our 'Diesel Greenhouse.'"

"One day Dick showed up with a book, *General Viticulture* I think it was called, and we applied the same principles as for other fruit. We took the California guidelines for spacing the vines and everything and sort of modified them for our climate."

Jim Maresh has been "Dick's grower" ever since, and he says of the other old-timers, "I was without a winery of my own. But I had enough on my plate. And anyway I was working with Dick, and he was a good winemaker."

From his mantel, Maresh brings down a small, elegant barrel, handmade by Dick's father, and a tall, slim-necked bottle with "Gewürztraminer" handwritten on the label. In that bottle is all that remains from Erath's very first crush. The significance of both arti-facts is obvious and moving.

"The first crush was in 1972, in Dick's basement. Dick changed our lives, and I guess we changed his," Maresh says. Maresh also says he changed Dick's life in another way, by introducing him to Cal Knudsen. Dick has a different version of meeting Knudsen — through letters, and later a visit at Tektronix — but Maresh's has a nice romantic quality.

Maresh says, "Cal Knudsen came here and said he was interested in growing grape vines. I later told Dick, 'Here's the guy we need.' He had money, and he was a sophisticated business man with vision and leadership qualities." According to Maresh, he and Knudsen drove up to see Dick, who was out pruning in his vineyard. "The Oregon wine industry would not be the same," he asserts, "if Cal Knudsen hadn't come up this road."

From the Vine Came the Grape

❦

Growers Jim Maresh and Arthur Weber

Nor would the industry be the same today if Maresh and other growers had not forced legislation to preserve their land for farming. Since the 1970s, when Oregon's innovative Land Conservation and Development Commission (LCDC) began setting strict standards for statewide land use and planning, private and commercial land developers have sought ways to nibble at the valley's increasingly precious farmland. Scars are still visible where, about ten years ago, a large quarry operation began chomping rock out of a hill just south of Maresh's Red Barn, adjacent to his vineyard.

"What a lot of people don't realize," Maresh says, "is that asphalt batch plants at quarries produce emissions that affect vineyards, which tend to soak up pollution like giant sponges. I'd seen what developers had done to the land in California and Nevada, so I went to the LCDC to see if I could get some rules to favor vineyards."

Fortunately, he arrived on a day the LCDC was to deal with a matter concerning the controversial and now-defunct Rajneesh commune in Eastern Oregon, and the press was out in full force. With a big grin, Maresh recounts, "For some reason they had to delay the main agenda item, and I got to be heard right away. Well, with all those television cameras and reporters we got a lot of attention, and soon after the state established zones for 'exclusive farm use' and protection against asphalt batch plants."

Maresh remembers, years ago, a less fortuitous press encounter. Dick was being interviewed about his vineyards, winery, and the future of the then budding wine industry. "As a farmer," Maresh says, "I go for tonnage. I had to learn that with grapes, less is better for good quality fruit — especially with Pinot Noir. Our vineyards now produce about two and one-half to three tons per acre, about like France, where it is controlled by the government. But when I started out, grapes were like any other fruit to me. That particular day, when Dick was getting interviewed by all these television people, I ran up all excited and said, 'Hey Dick! I'm getting six tons per acre!' All he did was sort of grimace and say, 'Keep it down!'"

Then there's the story about chicken manure and Chardonnay. "Well," Maresh says, "I planted Chardonnay vines over there behind the Red Barn. The vines went all over and the grapes weren't good, like they were sick or something, and I called up a guy at Oregon State University and asked if he could take a look at things. He came out but couldn't figure out what was wrong — until I told him that I used to pile chicken manure there. That was it. Those young vines and grapes just went crazy with all that rich fertilizer.

"At least until they got used to it," he adds with a smile. "Now we've got Chardonnay grapes back there the size of plums, and we use chicken manure in all our vineyards."

Jim talks about the soil, the microclimates and how they vary from ridge to ridge, how the frost runs downhill into the valley, and how the hills are frost-free from the middle of March to mid-November. "Pinot Noir vines grow deeper and are more complex. You need about two thousand heat units to ripen Pinot Noir. So you want to pick by mid-October, before the rains start, when the sugar is up and the acid down. The best weather is warm days and cold, snappy nights, when Mother Nature is saying: 'Hey! I've got to shut down. Get the grapes off before the big freeze!'"

Maresh talks about the great years recently, and hopes the weather doesn't reverse itself, and explains how the valley never developed a wine industry because the old-timers were conservative and religious. George Fox College, a Quaker institution, is in Newberg, only a few miles away from Dundee. Newberg was a "dry" town until fairly recently. During the days of early settlement, there were myriad strict religious and cult communities throughout the valley.

With the rain looking like it will keep coming down for at least forty more days and nights, Maresh says we might as well brave it. He wants to show me the inside of his Little Red Barn. So we slog on down in our rain gear. Maresh seems to mellow in the tasting room, which even on a gray day has a nice *gemütlichkeit* about it. The views are out into the mist, to the vineyards and the quarry scrapings beyond. Papers, bottles and glasses are scattered about as if a party has just broken up.

I see a picture of a Navy jet fighter, its pilot loading cases of wine into the bow. Jim laughs and tells me the pilot is his oldest son, David, a graduate of Annapolis who was once intelligence officer aboard the carrier USS *Eisenhower*. Now a full Navy captain, David has pleased his father by saying he would like to return and get involved in the farm.

Some of the Navy's top admirals have gathered up here on Worden Hill Road, far from anywhere, to drink Maresh's wine. "It got started when ships came into Portland during the Rose Festival," he explains. "Some of the officers wanted to come out for a wine tasting, and pretty soon word got out to the fleet. I once had five admirals up here drinking wine."

Healthy and vigorous at seventy-one, Jim says, "Every day, even though I'm retired, I've got to have a goal. It keeps me young. I work along with the Mexicans out there." He indicates the crew pruning vines, moving through the drizzle like subaqueous creatures. Mexican crews are omnipresent in Oregon vineyards. "Without the Mexicans," Jim adds, "the whole Oregon wine industry wouldn't have developed. They work hard, and not only that, they're creative. They know what they're doing."

After showing me his bottles and labels and the "attack frog" that sits on the barrels in his storage room, Maresh's eyes wander off to where men find pleasant reflections. Seeking more insight, I ask once again about Erath.

Maresh says quickly, "Dick Erath is probably one of the most generous men I've ever known. He's completely honest, and our deals have always been based on a handshake. At first, Dick and I were living out of each other's pockets. I'd be broke and need money, and he might say to me, 'How'd you do in the tasting room?' Then he might give me five hundred dollars in advance of my crop."

I mention others, and Maresh says, "Dave Lett was different, more reticent, more of a loner. And Chuck Coury, well, he always wanted

*From the Vine
Came the Grape*

❦

*Growers Jim Maresh
and Arthur Weber*

to be a leader but never had enough followers. But listen, all these guys were good guys. But when I see a battered car coming up the road and know it's Dick Erath, it makes me feel good. Dick has so much talent. He's an engineer, a photographer, a ham radio operator — but deep down he's a farmer. He'd rather be out in his vineyard than in the lab, like a lot of winemakers. We're succeeding because of Dick's knowledge, and he's the same person who first came up to my door. He hasn't changed a bit."

Despite years of struggle, Jim Maresh remains content in his own life and marriage. "The wine industry is a graveyard for marriages," he says, naming no one, "but Loie and I have been together for forty-eight years. Winemakers tend to become obsessed, immersed in the industry, which isn't that lucrative at first. There's a lot of sacrifice for that 'great dream.'"

"You know," he concludes, "in a way, my wife and I were pioneers. We always wanted to do something different, and the best decision we ever made was coming to Oregon."

ARTHUR WEBER

Arthur Weber and his wife, Vivian, live below Worden Hill Road in a renovated farmhouse at the bottom of a long private drive, beside an ancient fir tree Weber calls "Big Doug." Below Big Doug, the land falls away in a view that reaches far out into the valley. The property above merges into a steep slope of the Dundee Hills. The vineyards are just west of the house, on a ridge running north and south with slopes to the east and west. Weber bought the property in two transactions, twenty-one acres in 1972, then sixty-five acres and the decaying house in 1976.

From Weber's wide porch, if the day is spring-clear and sunny like this one, you can spot Dick Erath's house atop his hill. Jim Maresh's home is also uphill, slightly to the northwest. Despite the proximity of these close friends and other houses along Worden Hill Road, Weber's property has a serene sense of isolation that makes the visitor want to linger, just looking off to where hawks are riding the thermals above the valley and hearing Big Doug catch the breeze.

The old farmhouse is spacious and warm, with dark wood left after much renovation and wide windows that let in even gray days. There are pictures of Indians, wildlife, and older and interesting places, and the refrigerator is covered with photographs of family and friends. The furniture is mostly antique. And there are other bibelots about, noticeably symbols, tokens, and talismans that represent pigs, humorous and otherwise. Have I stumbled into some arcane swine cult?

I ask about the pigs and Weber laughs heartily. He is sixty-two and a big man, a former football player grown thinner because of a recent intestinal ailment. His humor is obviously undiminished by his illness. "Yeah, the pig thing. Well, when I had my fortieth birthday I got this pig for a gift—a real one that we raised and later ate. Ever since, on any occasion, people have been giving me pig gifts as a kind of joke. Now they're all over the place. But," he adds, "I do like pigs."

Looking past Weber's shoulder, I can see Erath's house on its hill. When I mention how it dominates the landscape like the lair of some feudal lord, he laughs again.

"I tell Dick I should charge him scenic easement rights because of his view of my vineyard," he says lightly, then explains that Erath's rights have already been confirmed by his long-term lease on thirty-two acres of Weber's eighty-six acres of land. In 1975, with Erath's help, Weber began planting Pinot Noir, Riesling, Pinot Gris and Chardonnay. The Riesling went in first, in 1975, and the Pinot Noir the following year. Currently, twenty of the leased acres are planted in Pinot Noir and the remaining twelve acres in the white varieties.

Weber's deep friendship with Erath was bonded in those early days, when they were struggling and worked side by side. "He was very helpful, supplying advice and plants and working for me by the hour. He was dirt poor then, but very astute. I think he's very near a genius, and he has helped me considerably."

Unlike Jim Maresh, Weber sells no wine. "I never wanted, ever, ever, to get into the wine business," he explains. "It's not in my makeup; I didn't have the necessary ego. You have to have a great ego to be a great winemaker." Years ago however, back in a much earlier life, Weber confesses that he had been an amateur winemaker who dreamed of someday making wine from his own grapes.

Erath laughs and remembers, "Yeah, the only time Weber tried making wine here he screwed up. It was a Pinot Noir and it was pretty thin, with a lot of what we call 'volatile acidity,' or 'v.a.' That's the smell of vinegar," he adds with another laugh, "not the Veteran's Administration. We kidded him and gave the wine an Italian name: Weberelli."

Weber was born in Hawaii. He was graduated with a degree in business from the University of Oregon in Eugene, where he was a star center linebacker on the football team, and where he began his love affair with Oregon. After leaving college, however, it took him a while to get back. He was a pilot in the Air Force stationed in Germany during the late 1950s and afterwards started a small publishing house in Boston.

"It was nothing exotic," Weber explains. "We published college math books. Later I sold the business and started an international publishing operation for the buyer on the West Coast. I had to get back out here. Every time I left Oregon, to go in the service, to work in Boston or whatever, I would say to myself, 'What am I doing?'"

Weber and Vivian were married in 1969, came to Oregon three years later, and, just like that, bought their first piece of land.

"Actually it was all because of Dave Lett. I had met Dave, who like me was once a book salesman, while we were selling textbooks at Oregon State University. Vivian and I had planned to go to Europe in 1972, but because I knew Lett was up here, we decided to come up and see him instead. I knew he was growing grapes and making wine, and I thought maybe he could help us check out the possibilities of getting a place of our own. I thought about buying some land in California, but land there was about five thousand dollars an acre, compared to five hundred here."

Looking for Lett, Weber stopped at a service station in Dundee to ask directions.

"The guy said, 'Sure, I know where he lives. But he told me if I told anyone he'd stop buying gas from me.' So I just turned up the hill on Ninth Street until I saw a 'Land for Sale' sign. That was the first twenty-four acres we bought from Jim Maresh. With no house on the property, we lived in a tent. Friends from all over the country visited us, bringing their own tents, until the number grew and we became known as 'Tent City.'"

While Weber considers Dave Lett a "curmudgeon," he holds no grudge about not finding him that fateful day.

"Dave Lett probably wouldn't admit it, but he's a lot like Charles Coury," Weber says, "And I've got to tell you a story about Coury. I had a friend who lived over near Forest Grove, near Coury's vineyard, and I decided to drop by. When I asked him if he might tell me a little bit about the business, he just looked at me and asked what I was going to pay him for consulting." He laughs. "He was irascible, yes, but not in an unpleasant way. He said to me, 'I know you're going to be around.' I considered that an encouragement."

Today, Weber is successful enough, and happy he says, sustained by his love of nature. He is a fly fisherman and bird watcher — a huge telescope is propped on the porch — and Vivian is busy working as a travel agent and completing a graduate degree in Spanish at Portland State University.

Vivian arrives, her arms full of books, and hears us talking about Erath.

"Joan is perfect for him," she asserts. "Dick and Art tend to be a lot alike. They have a tendency to run over women. They need someone to stand up to them. Dick's very social, but he's humble and shy with strangers. He's also a great cook."

After some comments on the egos and obsessions of grape growers, winemakers and the trouble with spouses, Vivian slips away to study. Weber grins after her. As the dust settles, he says, "I've always prided myself on staying away from becoming caught up in too much success. And with Dick, we're close friends and I've never let business get in the way of our friendship. We've always maintained a bond, and his boys have been like surrogate sons to me."

Weber is quiet for a moment, reflecting. "There's no question in my mind that here, in the Dundee Hills, is one of the ten top places in the world for growing grapes. Or, arguably, one of the six top places. It's right up there.

"And you know what?" he says, "I can't believe I'm sitting in one of the best wine regions in the world. It never fails to amaze me."

The winemakers of Yamhill County, October 1983 (clockwise from lower left): Joe Campbell, Bill Blosser, Don Bynard, Myron Redford, Dick Erath, Fred Arterberry, Fred Benoit, David Lett, David Adelsheim.

Today and Tomorrow

Today, as the Oregon wine industry completes its first twenty-five years,
theories abound about the industry's future. As the industry
grows rapidly and more aggressive entrepreneurs arrive to compete
for land and resources, particularly in the Willamette Valley, some
wonder whether Oregon will be able to maintain its tradition of small
and elegant wineries.

As larger corporate operations enter the field, some worry that
exigencies of mass-market winemaking — the production of low-
priced volume wines — may tarnish the hard-won reputation of Oregon wines. Others believe Oregon can support wineries of all
sizes, and that the smaller "boutique" wineries will be able to co-exist
alongside larger newcomers. All agree, however, that after all the
remarkable achievements of the past twenty-five years, the industry
may look forward to a bright and limitless future.

Oregon Wine Advisory Board (OWAB) figures indicate that between
1986 and 1996 the number of wineries in Oregon grew from forty-
seven to 116. Oregon wine sales increased 272 percent. Figures for
1996 indicate that Oregon ranks second in the nation, just behind
California, in number of wineries. It ranks fourth in the nation in total
production, with an output of 750,000 cases. Of that production,
sixty-two percent is red wine, mostly Pinot Noir, and thirty-eight
percent is white. From some 5,800 acres of vinifera grapes harvested
in 1996 (out of a state total of 7,500 acres planted), major wine
varieties produced were: Pinot Noir, Chardonnay, Riesling, Pinot
Gris, Cabernet Sauvignon, Müller-Thurgau, Gewürztraminer.

More important to the OWAB, which is under the aegis of the Oregon Department of Agriculture, wine sales totaled ninety million dollars in 1996. That represents a benefit of more than one hundred million dollars to the state's economy.

The OWAB, formed in 1983, is supported by wine industry taxes. In turn, OWAB spends one-third of its annual budget ($500-750 thousand) to support industry research at Oregon State University. Oregon growers pay the highest grape tax in the world, twenty-five dollars per ton, annually. A smaller amount of revenue comes from a "privilege tax" paid by all wineries, in- or out-of-state, that produce more than one hundred thousand gallons per year and sell their product in Oregon. In 1996, that tax was sixty-seven cents a gallon, of which two cents went to the OWAB and the remainder was divided between the Oregon Department of Mental Health and the General Fund.

Officially, the wine board's principle task is the promotion and marketing of "Oregon's enological products." This is done through the International Pinot Noir Celebration, the Oregon State Fair, Oregon Public Broadcasting's "Grape Performance" and other activities, including seminars, auctions and expositions.

International marketing, which got into full gear in the late 1980s, is done in affiliation with the wine industries of Washington and Idaho. Leading trading partners, in order of importance, are Canada, the United Kingdom, Europe and Asia. In the past several years, exports have grown exponentially—from about eight percent in the 1980s to some thirty percent in 1996.

Barney Watson, Senior Instructor of Enology at Oregon State University in Corvallis and a well-respected consultant to the industry, draws a good portion of his salary from OWAB. Watson, now in his late forties, earned his master's degree in viticulture and enology at Davis and was teaching there when he was asked to come to Oregon in 1976.

Many of Oregon's early winemakers got to know Watson while attending classes at Davis. He is also a winemaker, which has helped him earn their trust. Watson and his wife, Nola Mosier, are partners in Tyee Wine Cellars, which they established in 1985 on an old farmstead in the Coast Range south of Corvallis. In 1996, Tyee produced thirty-five thousand cases of "handcrafted" Pinot Gris,

Pinot Noir, Chardonnay, Pinot Blanc and Gewürztraminer.

Today Watson sees himself in a crucial role not only as an advisor and consultant, but as a teacher. He hopes to inspire a new generation of Oregon winemakers, perhaps guiding them towards careers in their own or others' vineyards.

Since 1975, the o s u Enology Program, which is part of the Department of Food Science and Technology, has grown from two to four faculty members, including Watson. Enrollment has doubled in the Fermentation Sciences Program —the study of production and analysis of wine, beer and spirits. Anticipating the industry's needs, Watson wants to fortify the program by expanding faculty and resources and acquiring additional funding.

Despite the burgeoning wine industry, Watson notes that Oregon is still "beer country." The state is the acknowledged "microbrew capital of the world," second only to Belgium in number of breweries per capita. And he points out that Oregon's wine output is minuscule compared to California's much larger and longer-established wineries, and negligible when compared to the rest of the world. With a knowing smile, he says, "All of our production last year could be compared to just one moderate-sized winery in the Napa Valley."

In 1996, California produced 2.1 million tons of grapes, while Oregon's production was only fifteen thousand tons. The future, however, will most certainly be different. According to o s u, the Willamette Valley has an estimated thirty-five thousand acres of potential vineyards, and Watson points out that these are being bought up by new players from California, France, Australia, Japan and elsewhere.

Like many others, Watson sees Pinot Noir remaining in the leading role, but envisions a greater role for Pinot Gris and Pinot Blanc, with inroads from new French clones of Chardonnay. "This whole business is one big experiment," Watson feels, "whether you're in France, where they've been making wine for thousands of years, or in Oregon, where we've been making it since yesterday. The old-timers were farsighted in emphasizing the need for research and evaluation, especially for Pinot Noir, over the long term."

Watson mentions internecine battles, several years ago, between those who wanted to keep the industry small and intimate and those who felt the future was in expansion and reaching out for new markets. "There's a paradox here," he says. "Most people don't want more competition, but they want more people to buy their wine. Nevertheless, Oregon premium wines are a real growth industry. While people may be drinking less, they are drinking better."

While much larger wineries are coming to Oregon now, some expect future growth to be predominantly among small (5,000 - 10,000 case) to medium-sized (10,000 - 20,000 case) wineries and believe that newcomers will adhere to the high standards of the pioneers.

Quality has always been a focus here. Since 1977, Oregon has had the highest vinifera wine standards in the United States. Wines must be no less than ninety percent of their labeled variety (compared to a U.S. average of seventy-five percent), and one hundred percent

Frank Prial, Terry Robards, Dick Erath, and Ed McCarthy drinking the last two bottles of 1972 Pinot Noir at Erath Vineyards' 25th Anniversary Celebration.

appellation, i.e., grapes from that specific region. Vintage wines must be ninety-five percent grapes from the vintage year.

Oregon winemakers concur that much of what is happening today will determine the industry's future direction. Larger corporate investments like Willamette Valley Vineyards, just south of Salem alongside the I-5 freeway, are accepted as inevitable. Willamette Valley Vineyards was funded by some five thousand Oregon enthusiasts who became shareholders in the $10.5 million venture. The state-of-the-art winery produces a whopping ninety thousand cases of wine a year (Pinot Noir, Chardonnay, Riesling, Müller-Thurgau and Pinot Gris), with future production estimated at as much as five hundred thousand cases annually.

Located adjacent to a popular theme park, with its huge gates and tower entrance highly visible from the freeway, Willamette Valley Vineyards has been described by detractors as "more Disney than Burgundy." Such sentiments reflect the "sour grapes" attitude of detractors opposed to large operations in general.

Other giants striding into the state include Benziger, William Hill, Archery Summit and Benton Lane. Of these, the biggest outside the Willamette Valley is King Estate Winery, southwest of Eugene, which has a goal of 170 thousand-case capacity. Current examples of foreign investment are Argyle Winery (The Dundee Wine Company), which is a partnership between Australian vintner Brian Croser and local grower Cal Knudsen, and the French-owned Domaine Drouhin Oregon (DDO). However, DDO's exclusivity, higher prices, low volume, and commitment to enhancing the Willamette Valley's reputation place it closer alongside Oregon's early winemakers.

Today and Tomorrow

❦

Growing Into the Future

A Battle for the Soul

THE FUTURE OF
THE OREGON WINE INDUSTRY

On those clear, hot days when the vineyards are green and the Willamette Valley sprawls out to a far distant haze, you can look down
from the Dundee Hills and still see room for dreams. Those who
came first, winemakers like Dick Erath and the other boys up north,
are still sharing dreams they brought with them twenty-five years
ago. Those dreams are now part of a tradition that well may endure,
as it has in the great wine regions of Europe, for centuries.

With newcomers entering the valley as pioneers have for 150 years,
making the land expensive and scarce, dreams are perhaps more important than ever before. Among old-timers, there is real concern that
newcomers to Oregon's wine industry, mercenaries arriving with little
more than clean hands and cool cash, might ultimately betray what
has always been most important here: the "search for the Holy Grail."

One early Oregon winemaker described it as "a battle for the soul
of Oregon's wine trade," and predicted a showdown between the
divergent philosophies of winemaking: the large, impersonally corporate against the smaller, more individualistic "boutique."

A quarter century of venerability confers respect and encourages
us to romanticize the pioneers who built the Oregon wine industry.
These romantics who came north to carve out vineyards in the Willamette Valley are not dissimilar to the pioneers who plodded the
Oregon Trail to homestead here. Each made a decision to leave the
familiar and secure. All were driven by amorphous dreams of creating new lives for themselves and their families and taking control of
their destinies.

From their travels and studies of winemaking, particularly in France, Oregon's wine pioneers were confident that the Willamette Valley would eventually be one of America's most important wine regions. After all, the valley's seasonal cycles and day lengths are similar to Burgundy's, as is its cool, wet weather. It provides a window in time compatible with the growing of certain select varieties, notably Pinot Noir — the noble grape of Burgundy.

These wine pioneers succeeded, brilliantly and in a short time, through a combination of commitment, perseverance and luck — that stuff often granted to beginners and, in the case of Oregon's beginning winemakers, those foolish enough to leave the comfortable warmth of California's time-proven valleys.

"Do I have luck?" Dick Erath asks dubiously. "Perseverance is a better word for it."

Oregon's early winemakers were literally and figuratively "babes in the woods." They knew little about farming. Most came from other professions, captivated by wine and winemaking. They loved the independence of it all, growing and creating it with their own hands. Some had studied theory at the University of California, others had hands-on experience here and abroad. Few were prepared for the challenges they faced on the way to harvesting and bottling their first vintage. At least it was never boring.

According to Mark Twain, "Life can be dangerous, but never serious." Winemaking, however, is a most serious art indeed. After all, the winemaker's opportunity to produce a good, perhaps outstanding, vintage comes but once a year. Usually this is the responsibility of one person, traditionally the owner of the vineyard. More recently, it is often the task of a hired winemaker who takes great pride in his or her skill.

Oregon's original winemakers have always been driven to excel, but not to better one another. Their quest has been for quality. "I don't compete with anyone else. I compete with myself," remains an axiom among the wine pioneers. Now, with its reputation firmly established worldwide, the Oregon wine industry would be embarrassed to have its brief but highly regarded tradition of excellence dishonored by high-volume, lower-quality wine production "by committee."

Some contend that larger commercial wineries will never be able to produce a quality Pinot Noir. Even detractors, however, have grudging admiration for Domaine Drouhin, which established its sizeable winery in the valley in 1988.

They are not, after all, the first French winemakers to practice their craft here. Early in the last century, pensioned-off French-Canadian employees of the Hudson's Bay Company established settlements not far from the Dundee Hills. Wine bottles have been discovered at the sites, and archeologists claim that evidence of wine bottles confirms the existence of vineyards, winemaking and, therefore, a "civilized community."

Now that the French have rediscovered this turf that matches many of the environmental attributes of their homeland, bringing with them centuries of tradition and skill reaching back to Roman times, their advantages are immeasurable. The happy surprise in this scenario is the respect and compatibility between the venerable French traditionalists and the brash Oregon winemakers who, at least early on, did it "on a wing and a prayer."

After only twenty-five years of wrestling with the vicissitudinous ways of Pinot Noir (and other varieties, as well), the respect is more than deserved. The French, among others, admire the Oregonians for coming up to the mark so quickly, and so well.

Their technologies may vary, but the French and the Oregonians are consistent in their demands for quality. More important, they agree that good wine is not made by formula.

The future, most concur, lies in the cultivation of new and imported grape clones and in making even greater Pinot Noirs. Some say Pinot Noir has just about reached state-of-the-art in Oregon. There is also a future in white wines. Erath believes that Pinot Gris and Pinot Blanc are true Oregon specialties that will gradually take the emphasis away from Chardonnay, now the most popular white wine locally and nationally.

Not all early Oregon winemakers foresee a future bleak with corporate exploitation. Some feel the newcomers have not only adapted the ways of the pioneers, but have begun to improve the industry through better winemaking and improved management, creating a "synergy" driven by new techniques of mass marketing and production.

All heavy stuff, of course, but reflecting an industry made vulnerable through transition. The future will determine whether Oregon's winemakers will continue their quest for the greatest Pinot Noir, or whether our vineyards and wineries will become debased, mass-culture tourist attractions sprawling throughout the valley —"and to hell with quality!"

In reality, Oregon's wine industry is guaranteed a successful future, and probably one not as dramatic or drastic as anyone predicts. In fact, the determining factor may not be wine alone, but an inextricable concern for the environment and Oregon's lifestyle.

This means that, whatever happens here during the next twenty-five years, we should assure ourselves that Oregon will remain a "last good place" — a place not only to cultivate grapes and make fine wine, but where the future provides plenty of room for dreams.

A NOTE ON THE TYPE

This book was set in Émigré Filosofia, a typeface drawn in 1996 in California by Zuzana Licko. Ms Licko, a Yugoslavian emigré to the United States, considers Filosofia her interpretation of the famous Moderns drawn by and named for Giambattista Bodoni di Parma in 1798. Its use here is an example of the way in which European culture—like wine—has migrated across the Atlantic in the imagination of its artisans to be reinvented within the context of the new world. This book was designed and set by The Felt Hat in Portland, Oregon.